W9-AHL-232

family history detective

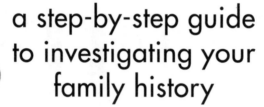 a step-by-step guide
to investigating your
family history

family history detective

desmond walls allen

FAMILY
TREE
BOOKS

Cincinnati, Ohio
shopfamilytree.com

Harrison County Public Library
Elizabeth Branch

Family History Detective. Copyright © 1998 and 2011 by Desmond Walls Allen. First published as First Steps in Genealogy: A Beginner's Guide to Researching Your Family History. Manufactured in the United States of America. All rights reserved. No part of this book may be reproduced in any form or by any electronic or mechanical means including information storage and retrieval systems without permission in writing from the publisher, except by a reviewer, who may quote brief passages in a review. Published by Family Tree Books, an imprint of F+W Media, Inc., 10150 Carver Road, Cincinnati, Ohio 45242. (800) 289-0963. Second edition.

ISBN: 978-1-14403-1687-6

First edition ISBN: 978-1-55870-489-3

A
929.1

Other Family Tree Books are available from your local bookstore and online suppliers. For more genealogy resources, visit <shopfamilytree.com>.

15 14 13 12 11   5 4 3 2 1

Distributed in Canada by Fraser Direct
100 Armstrong Avenue
Georgetown, Ontario, Canada L7G 5S4
Tel: (905) 877-4411

Distributed in the U.K. and Europe by F&W Media International, LTD
Brunel House, Forde Close,
Newton Abbot, TQ12 4PU, UK
Tel: (+44) 1626 323200,
Fax (+44) 1626 323319
E-mail: enquiries@fwmedia.com

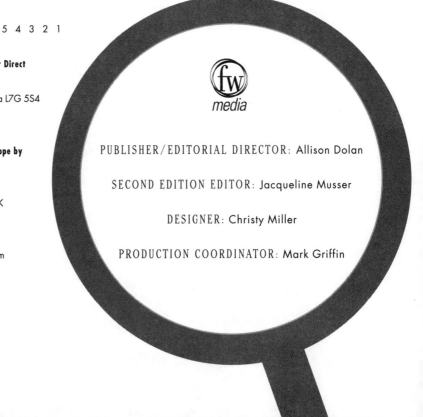

PUBLISHER/EDITORIAL DIRECTOR: Allison Dolan

SECOND EDITION EDITOR: Jacqueline Musser

DESIGNER: Christy Miller

PRODUCTION COORDINATOR: Mark Griffin

About the Author

Desmond Walls Allen has taught seminars and workshops on genealogical topics for twenty-five years. She is the owner of Arkansas Research, Inc., a historical and genealogical publishing company devoted to Arkansas resources. She appeared as a guest expert in the first PBS *Ancestors* series, and has hosted Arkansas Educational Television Network's *Researching Your Family Tree*. Desmond is the author, compiler, or editor of 237 books. She has written many articles on genealogical and historical research methods. And she's a member of MENSA, the international organization for people who have IQs in the 98th percentile and above.

Dedication

Martha Vaughn, aka Patsy the Witch. This photo of Patsy the Witch was taken around 1900 when Patsy was in her early nineties. A distant cousin of mine—also a descendant of Patsy—sent me the picture. Don't be afraid to contact relatives you only just discovered—they may want to share information as much as you do!

Acknowledgments

My ancestor, Martha "Patsy the Witch" Vaughn, deserves credit for my initial interest in genealogy. My great-grandmother told me about her great-grandmother, a woman who could predict the future, cast spells, and change people into animals. Patsy the Witch dangles at the bottom of my pedigree chart—her line is my maternal one, the whole way. I found her and her maternal grandmother as well.

This book wouldn't have been possible without the people from whom I learned research methods and all those students I, in turn, taught to do genealogy. The questions and stories from my students helped me decide what novice genealogists need to know.

My sincerest appreciation goes to my mother, Elizabeth O. Williams Walls, for her unconditional love and encouragement. My son, Hadley Edward Hirrill, and granddaughter, Hali Elizabeth Hirrill, continue to inspire me to research and write about our family.

The first edition of this book was written in 1998, and I'm astonished at how much has changed in the field of genealogy since then and now (2011) with the second edition. The Internet, with its tremendous resources and the opportunity it presents to connect people, is an amazing thing.

TABLE OF *contents*

introduction

I wrote this book from a selfish standpoint, and I thought perhaps you'd like to know why. When I first started on my family history pursuit, I thought of it as a search for *my* ancestors. Through the years, I discovered the people who turned up in my pedigree aren't just *my* ancestors—they're the ancestors of lots of folks. My ancestors may be *your* ancestors. And if you'll get busy and involve yourself in the research process, perhaps you'll solve some of the problems about our ancestors I haven't been able to.

I used to write a genealogy column for a newspaper, so I received lots of interesting mail. One researcher wrote, saying he was positively alarmed about the number of his ancestors when he did the mathematical computation to learn how many ancestors were back there. He knew he had two parents, four grandparents, eight great-grandparents, and so on. So he took pencil in hand and started working out how many ancestors he was descended from in the one hundredth generation. (Go ahead, try this yourself. Your calculator won't handle the final results, so be prepared to do math the old-fashioned way.)

My correspondent got back to ten generations with his pencil and figured he was

descended from 1,024 people in that generation. I can imagine a crowd of that size; you probably can, too. But when he reached twenty generations, he counted over a million people—slightly less than the current population of the entire state of Maine. If you don't get bogged down in the zeros, work back to 100 generations and you'll arrive at a number that boggles the mind. I had to use an encyclopedia to determine what numbers that large are called. The figure is 1,267,700,000,000,000,000, 000,000,000,000. In layperson's terms, that's a little over 1.2 nonillion ancestors in the 100th generation.

The *Oxford American Dictionary* estimates a generation as thirty years. So one hundred generations would put us back to about 1000 B.C. Then we arrive at a problem—there weren't that many people on the earth. (And those were only his ancestors.) The population of the world in 1650 was only about 500 million people.

Where had his thinking gone astray? He isn't descended from 1.2 nonillion different people who were exclusively *his* ancestors. He is the product of one hundred generations of intermarriage among the world's population. If you have New England ancestry, you'll probably discover many of your lines go back to just a few ancestral couples who came over in the seventeenth century. Their descendants intermarried.

The United States is a country on the move. We don't stay in the same location for dozens of generations like people of other countries did in historic (and prehistoric) times. So our pedigree charts are fairly diverse. But it isn't always so. Several years ago, the news media ran stories about a man in an English village whose DNA matched that of a prehistoric skeleton. The stories said he was probably related to most of the people in the town. And some of us whose ancestors left that town for America a couple of hundred years ago are probably related to that skeleton, too.

It's when we begin to see the big picture and think about all those ancestors of ours who wove the fabric of our pedigree that we realize we're all part of a global family.

So, cousin, start working on your family history research. Be sure to read the chapter on sharing your family history research, because I want to know what you find out about *our* family.

It's ubiquitous, it's indexed, it
But once you've been researching f
you start lamenting the 10-year ga
census records and curse the missing 189
It sure would be easier to keep tabs o

STEP 1

WHERE'D YOU GET THOSE EYES?
The Why, What, and How of Family History

Look in the mirror: Everything you see came from your ancestors—your eyes, the shape of your face, the length of your nose, and a hundred other features staring back at you. You inherited personality traits, disease predispositions, and thousands of features you can't see. Who are you? You're the product of your ancestors' gene pool. Scary thought? Perhaps it's time for you to learn more about all those people who contributed to your makeup.

WHY

Think about *why* you want to know about your ancestors. Your interest in genealogy may come from ordinary curiosity about all the people who contributed to who you are. Genealogy research is not just about your ancestors—it's about self-discovery. You'll learn more about yourself when you hit the pedigree trail.

If you're curious about your ancestors, you've probably reached the point in your life where you can turn inward. When people are young, they're often preoccupied with earning a living and rearing children. Somewhere in the growth process, your thoughts become introspective. You begin to want answers to questions such as, "Why am I like I am?"

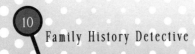

Perhaps you have a medical problem and wonder if something in your genetic makeup contributed to the situation. You can learn who your ancestors were, and attempt to discover their causes of death. We're reading more and more in the news about the importance of genetic research, and you may wonder where your genes came from and whether or not you may have inherited tendencies that leave you vulnerable to particular diseases.

Maybe you've heard family stories, legends, and mysteries and want to learn more about them. With ongoing interest in the Civil War, you may want to find out who your ancestors were who served in that war. Or you might want to join a lineage society like the Daughters of the American Revolution or Mayflower Descendants. If you're descended from or related to a famous ancestor, your research may take you in that direction.

Possibly you want a hobby that brings your family members together. Young people are natural computer users and bring energy and enthusiasm to a new interest.

Your interest may not be from self-interest at all. Perhaps you want to help someone with a school project. Social studies teachers often assign genealogical projects. Or you may want to do some research about someone else's family as a gift or reward. Perhaps your grandmother-in-law is in failing health and needs someone to do her "legwork" on her genealogy research. Or possibly you're going on vacation to an area where your neighbors' ancestors lived, and they want you to "just drop into the courthouse" for them.

Whatever your motivation, you'll be hooked on this hobby once you experience a little success. And that's what this book is about—your success.

WHAT

What do you want to know? If you start on your search expecting to find only positive things about your ancestors, you may be in for a surprise. Ancestors had an odd habit of being human.

Do you just want to know the names of your ancestors? Will a pedigree chart listing your direct ancestors be enough to satisfy your curiosity?

Probably you'll want to learn as much as you can about all your ancestors as far back in time as possible. And you'll want to know about your entire family, not just the people you're descended from. Those atrocious aunts, colorful cousins, and unique uncles can add spice to your family history.

HOW

You know why you want to know; you know what you want to know; now let's take care of how you'll find out. This book is designed to set you on the right path to begin your genealogical research. It isn't the only book you'll need on the subject, and it doesn't contain everything you'll need to know. But it will get you headed in the right direction.

Keep two concepts in mind as you wade into the research process:
- How you know is as important as what you know.
- Your search isn't just about names; it's about people.

> Genealogy isn't just about collecting information; it's about analyzing and evaluating what you find.

From the beginning, keep track of the sources of your information—you'll be glad you did later on. Genealogy isn't just about collecting information; it's about analyzing and evaluating what you find. And to do that, you have to know where your information came from.

With all of today's databases of names, it's possible to lose sight of your objective and turn genealogy into a search for names. Your ancestors were much more than names in a database. They were living, breathing human beings who were born, lived their lives, and died. They didn't exist in a vacuum—they were part of a community, part of larger groups of people.

First we need to talk about what traits will make you a good genealogical researcher. It's helpful to be adventurous, analytical, consistent, courteous, creative, curious, determined, patient, skeptical, and well organized. If this description doesn't completely fit you now, it's still possible for you to become a very good genealogist, but you may have to develop some of these traits along the way.

The place to begin is with yourself. Your search for ancestors is about you. You may want to keep a journal or write your autobiography. Begin your search for information in your home. Raid the refrigerator for those stories that have been in cold storage all these years. Visit family cemeteries.

Before you overwhelm yourself with information, organize your facts. We'll offer suggestions for creating group sheets and pedigree charts, and filing your papers. Correspondence, now more electronic than traditional, may become a big part of your routine. Computer software offers the best way to shape your facts into manageable form.

Your computer may become your new best friend. After you mine the Internet for information, your search will take you to libraries and archives. You'll look online and in libraries for previously published books and articles about your family lines, and search for newly found cousins who may be working on the ancestors you have in common with them. With the Internet, it's easier than ever to make those connections.

Bread and butter, Fred Astaire and Ginger Rogers, history and genealogy; some things just go together. In order to understand your ancestors, you can learn about the times in which they lived. The political, social, economic, and geographic history of the time and place where they lived can give you insights into what they did and why they did it.

Then we'll dive into federal census records, a mainstay of genealogical research. Imagine a nationwide photo—the federal government took one every ten years. The other most-used set of records for genealogists comes from courthouses where your ancestors went to do their day-to-day business. You'll learn how to access census and courthouse records.

After you've accumulated information, evaluated it, analyzed what it means, and organized it, you'll probably want to share what you've learned with other members of your family. You can rally your cousins and stage a family reunion. Perhaps you'll join genealogical societies, or create a home page on the Internet featuring your genealogical information.

At the end of this book, you'll find a family group sheet and pedigree forms. These will help you organize your ancestors. A research calendar form will help you organize your searches. You'll find a glossary to explain unfamiliar terms. Any new field of study has its own language; we'll help with the ones you'll encounter in genealogy. We've supplied some addresses in our resource directory. All along the way in this book, we encourage you to say how you know what you know. Source citation is important, so we've supplied examples for you to follow.

The important fact is you've begun your search for your family history by picking up this book. You've taken the first step! In the following chapters, you'll learn about starting a successful genealogical search.

KEY CLUES

- Remember you're researching real people, not just names and dates.
- Start your search for your ancestors with yourself.
- Organize your facts.
- Connect with fellow researchers online.
- Brush up on your history to better understand your ancestors' lives.

PLAYING SHERLOCK HOLMES
The Genealogist's Skills and Goals

Before you start on your search for ancestors, let's examine your skills. You're motivated to start your quest for ancestors; after all, you've picked up this book. There are some skills that can assist your research. You probably already have most of them.

Here's a hint—and keep this in mind as you read through this chapter. If you're great at research, but not good at organization or correspondence, then enlist the aid of one of your siblings, or your spouse, or a cousin. If you love using the computer and corresponding with people, but don't enjoy tramping through a cemetery, use the buddy system to get the work done. Team up with someone who is good at the things you aren't. Involve your children and grandchildren in your search—seeing it through their eyes will give you a new perspective.

HELPFUL SKILLS
INQUISITIVENESS
Sherlock Holmes would have made a good genealogist. A keen, inquiring mind and a sense of adventure are essential. As you learn more from interviews, records, and reading, always ask "Why?"

and think about where new information will lead. Don't stop with a single document, follow the tracks it leaves. A death certificate may take you to funeral home records, newspaper obituaries, census schedules, military service and pension records, employment records, marriage licenses, probate court documents, and more.

CRITICAL THINKING

Critical thinking skills are essential. You must learn to question the validity of the sources you uncover. Is the death certificate correct? Does it match other known facts? Who gave the information that appears on the document? Is that person likely to be biased or have a reason for giving incorrect information?

Even published family histories you find about your ancestors may not be accurate. Just because something is in print doesn't make it so, and you must learn to evaluate the accuracy of the stories you hear and records you find.

ORGANIZATIONAL ABILITY

Organizational skills are very helpful to a genealogist. You might be a great detective and locate all kinds of information, but you must be able to organize the materials you find both physically and in your mind. Good record-keeping skills will help you pursue genealogy. The ability to take notes and write summaries of your research results will help you tremendously.

AVID READERS

Avid readers make better family historians. All the reading you've done of everything from history books to mystery novels will increase your understanding in your search. And to learn more about successful research methods, you need to read books and articles about how to find your ancestors. But then, you've already taken the first step in that direction, haven't you?

LISTENING

Developing the art of listening can do wonders for your genealogy. Listen to reference librarians, more experienced genealogists, and your older relatives. Some people ask a question, then concentrate on formulating their next question instead of listening to the answer to their original question. Digest answers. Listen for nuances of meaning. If your great-aunt hesitates when you ask about Grandma's first marriage, is it because she doesn't remember the details, or is it because she's deciding how much she should tell you about it? Give her a minute; look expectant. Don't speak just to fill the silence. Really listen with your whole body.

Listen to documents, too. Don't just read a marriage record and copy the facts from it. Listen to it. The record is saying two people decided to take a momentous step in their lives. Why did they do it? Who were their family and friends who supported their decision? Where did the marriage take place? Was there a celebration after the ceremony? Where did they plan to live? Listen to documents.

Harrison County Public Library
Elizabeth Branch

CONSISTENCY

Consistency is a good thing for genealogists. Take dates, for example. How many ways can you write your birthdate? July 25, 1950; 07/25/50; 25 July 1950; the twenty-fifth of July, nineteen hundred and fifty; 7.25.50; 19500725; 25/7/50. And these are just some of the possibilities. In genealogical circles, the "standard" format for writing a date is 25 July 1950, what some folks refer to as "military style." The day of the month comes first, followed by the month spelled as a word, then the year as a four-digit number.

Be consistent not only with dates, but with number formats, name conventions, and your note-taking.

There are exceptions to this practice. If you're copying dates from a written or published source, don't change the format—copy them just as you find them. One genealogist painstakingly transcribed old Quaker (Society of Friends) records and changed the dates she found there to the standard genealogical format. Dates in the record were expressed in the form "3.1.1742." Later, she found that Quakers, like many other English groups, started their year with March as the first month.

Be consistent not only with dates, but with number formats, name conventions, and your note-taking. If you consistently write the citation for your source in your notes before you examine it, you'll be much less likely to come away from a library with a sheet of notes from some unknown book, and wonder later where it came from. If you consistently copy names just as you find them, even when they're abbreviated, you won't wonder later whether the name was actually "Joseph" in the record and you were in a hurry and jotted down "Jos." or whether the name was "Jos." in the record.

SKEPTICISM

A healthy dose of skepticism is good for any genealogist. Just because Aunt Mozelle says it doesn't make it so. If you hear a tale about your family's descent from royalty, or a missed opportunity for a fabulous fortune, or something else that sounds a bit fantastic, reserve judgment about it and search for corroborating evidence.

Skepticism is one of those traits that defines your level as a researcher. As a beginner, you tend to believe everything you're told, even the bizarre stories. "Grandma lived to be 115 years old"—that sort of thing. After you progress a bit, and develop a little skepticism, you learn to interpret that as "Grandma probably lived to be very old." But do write down everything you're told, no matter how incredible it seems. And note who told you or where you read it. You'll probably find some grain of truth in the tale.

COURTESY

Courtesy goes a long way in genealogical pursuits. The old adage, "you can catch more flies with honey than with vinegar," applies to catching ancestors as well. Librarians, record custodians, and other people in public positions respond positively to smiles and expressions of appreciation. Your relatives will, too.

PATIENCE

Patience will make your search more enjoyable. It used to be hard to wait for the reply to a letter, now it's difficult to wait for the reply to an e-mail. If the clerk only knew how important that marriage record is to you—perhaps she'd hurry! You want to know who your ancestors were and you want to know now. Practice a little patience. If you don't receive a response to an inquiry in a timely manner, ask again. Maybe your e-mail disappeared in its travel through cyberspace. Some libraries and agencies routinely take a long time to respond. The New York vital records office often takes nine months to send a death certificate.

CREATIVITY

Be creative. Do try conventional methods first, but be open to unusual ideas. Use your personal frame of reference. You know your life is involved with groups of people; your ancestors' lives were, too. You may belong to labor organizations, business groups, religious bodies, trade unions, retired military associations, college fraternities or sororities, social clubs, softball teams, bowling leagues, Elvis fan clubs, or any of hundreds of others. Your ancestors were part of groups, too. They interacted with other people, and the records on those folks may help you find your family.

VISION

Think expansively. Being able to see the "big picture" will help you find your ancestors. You're probably part of a large family, even if you're an only child, when you include your spouse's relatives, ex-spouse's relatives, first cousins, aunts and uncles, and grandparents. Your extended family may include your brother-in-law's parents and family. Or the family of your grandmother's second husband. Your ancestors were part of interconnected family alliances, too. Keep your family members with known groups of associates and you'll have better chances for success in finding that elusive previous residence if you'll follow a group of people backward in time instead of a single family.

EXTROVERSION

Be an extrovert. After you've done genealogical research for a while, you'll realize we're all part of one big worldwide family. Potential cousins are everywhere. Develop an interest in other people's genealogy. In the chapter on courthouse research, you're cautioned not to bore the county clerk or the staff with stories about your ancestors. But it doesn't hurt to ask about their ancestors. One researcher asked a deputy clerk about her ancestors and learned they shared a great-great-grandmother.

IS THIS YOU?

Do you have any or all of these traits and skills that are helpful to genealogists? Are you an adventurous person with an inquiring mind? Are you an organized, consistent person who reads a lot and applies critical-thinking skills? Are you a patient, courteous person who listens well? Are you a

After you've done genealogical research for a while, you'll realize we're all part of one big worldwide family.

Creative Methods Pay Off: Finding Grandma Jackson's Grave

George began his search for his ancestors with only a little family information. He knew his mother, Zeffie, had been reared by her maternal grandmother, a woman known to the family simply as "Grandma Jackson." Her first name was lost to George's generation and his mother had died years ago. He knew Grandma Jackson had lived in western Arkansas, and the only remarkable thing he could remember from relatives' tales was that she had twins named "Lige" and "Bige." It wasn't much to go on.

Zeffie's mother, Alice, had died shortly after the birth of her third child, and the three children had been deserted by their father, Walter Owens, and left in the care of Grandma Jackson. Some simple guesswork and math pinpointed the time period in question as around the turn of the century, because George's mother was born in 1899. George's older sisters remembered their mother's childhood, but not her teen years, had been spent with her grandmother.

A trip to the library and a search of the 1910 federal census schedules for Arkansas turned up the three Owens children in the home of an uncle, Sam Jackson. But no Grandma Jackson. Figuring that Grandma Jackson must have died before the census was taken in 1910, a search in the old newspaper issues on microfilm was George's next step. Reading the newspapers told him a lot about the community in which his family had lived. It also turned up a 1909 obituary for Grandma Jackson. The story in the paper told about her good character, her death, the final illness, and described her funeral right down to the names of the songs that were sung. But she was referred to only as "Grandma" Jackson. An obituary in a newspaper published in a neighboring town mentioned that her burial had taken place in Blackfork Cemetery.

A search of the 1900 federal census revealed a Margaret Jackson in a western Arkansas county. She had twin sons in her home listed as "Elijah" and "Abijah." They had to be Lige and Bige. Grandma had a first name at last.

It was time for a field trip. George called the funeral home in the county seat of Polk County, Grandma Jackson's place of residence, to learn the location of Blackfork Cemetery. The cemetery was small and located in a remote area. But it was well cared for. George examined every gravestone, but didn't find one for Grandma Jackson. He found names of Grandma Jackson's neighbors he recognized from the census pages. He even found one for a Jackson child that must have belonged to one of Grandma's sons. But no Grandma.

Discouraged, scratched by briars, and bitten by chiggers, he was ready to give up. Then he had a creative idea. He wrote a note asking for anyone with information about Grandma Jackson's grave to please call him, and he left the card with his name and phone number in a sandwich bag tied to the cemetery's gatepost. He was confident, since the cemetery was obviously mowed on a regular basis, that people still cared about the graves there. He hoped the cemetery caretaker or other visitors might know where Grandma was buried.

Months went by before the cemetery caretaker called. She didn't know where Grandma Jackson was buried, but she supplied the name of a Jackson relative who might know. That led George to a previously unknown cousin from Oklahoma who had been present at Grandma Jackson's burial. Though only a child at the time, she remembered where her grandmother had been buried. She agreed to meet George at the cemetery and show him the grave. The grave was marked, but only with a large rock, not a tombstone. George later arranged to have a large marble gravestone erected for her. Grandma Jackson—found at last, thanks to a creative step in genealogical research.

Postscript: George didn't stop with Grandma, of course. He followed the Jackson family back into colonial North Carolina. Grandma Jackson's maternal line, the Hunter family, took him to seventeenth-century Virginia. Newly discovered cousins shared photographs, not only of Grandma Jackson, but of long-forgotten Grandpa Jackson as well.

creative extrovert who sees the big picture? You'll make an excellent genealogist. If this description doesn't fit you, remember that you can learn these skills and acquire these traits. And you can team up with a fellow researcher whose personality and abilities complement yours.

LINKING GENERATIONS

Genealogy isn't just about finding your ancestors, you must find those records connecting the people to parents in successive generations. One misstep in making those links may send you off on someone else's family line.

Use DNA testing in conjunction with your ancestors' paper trails. We can definitely establish parentage and define relationships among living people with DNA testing. Y-chromosome studies let us follow male lines into the ancient past. Research on mitochondrial DNA, the DNA passed from mother to daughter, though not as specific as that for Y-chromosomes, is becoming increasingly more popular.

So we have to evaluate all the data we find. And we're obligated to look for all the records about a particular subject, not just the ones that are easy to find or the ones that say what we want to believe. Then we must analyze the information we've found in our sources, and interpret what we've found.

Even then, we may be wrong. Genealogy is about people, and sometimes they behave just like human beings, not subjects in a scientific study. The father in a record may not be the biological father. Sometimes we find information that concerns, shocks, dismays, or embarrasses us. It's all part of our family's history. We can't change it; we just have to accept what we find, and continue our search, one generation at a time.

Genealogy Is About People

Nancy had been curious about her family history for a long time, but she was a busy elementary school teacher and didn't have time to do any serious research until she retired. She knew the man she'd called "daddy" was her stepfather, and that she came from her mother's first marriage. Her stepfather had been a wonderful man, and she'd always hesitated to ask questions about her biological father, because she didn't want her "daddy" to think there was something lacking in their relationship. Her stepfather had died by the time Nancy retired, and she decided she would ask her mother about her "real" father. But Nancy's mother was unwilling to discuss her first marriage.

Without her mother's help, Nancy started her search based on the information from her birth certificate. That document gave her father's name as John Underwood, and his birthplace as Illinois. She knew from looking at her mother's scrapbooks that the couple had been members of a traveling group of theatrical performers during the late 1920s when tent-shows featuring dramatic plays were as popular as movies are today. Nancy found a marriage record for her parents and learned from a newspaper clipping they'd been married in a newspaper office in one of the towns where their troupe was performing. The marriage had helped generate some publicity for the show. She also found a divorce record for the couple filed not long after her birth.

With the information she'd discovered, Nancy asked volunteers in the local genealogy group for help in locating her father in the federal census schedules for 1920, the most recent then available to researchers. She was able to find Underwood in the 1910 and 1900 census records.

Urged by her friends in the genealogy group, Nancy approached her mother with the information she'd found in the records about her father's family. Faced with Nancy's continued interest in family history, her mother revealed that Underwood wasn't Nancy's father at all. She had been married to Underwood, but did have an affair with another man while Underwood was employed with a different group of actors.

Nancy's mother told her who her true biological father was. Then Nancy remembered visits during her childhood from an Aunt Jewel and Uncle Dave, though she never knew her exact relationship to them. Her mother told her Uncle Dave was her father and Aunt Jewel was Dave's sister. They had stayed in touch with Nancy's mother until Nancy was a young married woman.

Nancy searched for more information and found Dave and Jewel were both deceased. Dave had married several years after Nancy's birth and had two children. Nancy was able to find them, and developed a rewarding, ongoing relationship with her newly found half-sister, Jerri. Jerri shared photos and stories with Nancy about their father, and gave her a volume of poetry and a painting created by their father. Nancy was later able to research her real father's family lines through traditional written records.

Nancy's voyage into family history took her into some rough seas. She was able to get on the right track because she maintained her curiosity, but at the same time respected her mother's feelings and didn't press her for information. After the breakthrough, Nancy's mother seemed relieved to be able to talk about her past. She and Nancy grew closer through the experience.

RESEARCH REPORTS

To prove the links between generations, we always hope to find documents that say Robert was the father of John. Modern vital records supply that kind of certainty. Wills, deeds, and court records that specifically mention relationships establish the links we're seeking. But sometimes we aren't lucky enough to find such straightforward sources. Then we have to gather all the information that exists about a particular family and attempt to interpret and analyze what we've found and make the best possible decision about whether Robert could be the father of John.

When you write this kind of report, you're helping yourself clarify your thoughts by putting them in written form.

As you accumulate, interpret, and analyze information about a family, it may become clear—to you, anyway—who the parents of an individual must have been. But it isn't enough just to know it, you must be able to tell others why you think so.

Put your thought processes in writing—think of it as a "thought experiment." List the pieces of evidence you've found and what they mean. List, as well, the sources you knew about but didn't have access to and couldn't search. Note the sources you searched that didn't produce any information. Use the citation guide at the end of this book to be sure you give complete information about your sources.

Argue with yourself on paper (well, in pixels perhaps); say what else the evidence could mean. Write about any evidence that points to a contrary possibility. If you're disagreeing with a written book or article, be sure to give a complete citation to the material.

Then write your conclusion. Your conclusion may be that you don't have enough information to make a decision about the point in question. Use the "Research Report" template supplied in the back of this book. What's the point of this step? Why create a report to yourself? Someday, you may want to tell a cousin why you reached a particular conclusion and if it's neatly laid out in a report, you won't have to re-create your thoughts. Your report may find a wider audience, especially if it's posted in some form on the Internet.

When you write this kind of report, you're helping yourself clarify your thoughts by putting them in written form. You're writing a reminder of sorts to yourself about the progress of your research. You may have to lay your work aside for a period of time, either until you can obtain access to the additional resources you need, or until you have time to return to your research.

CITING SOURCES

We can't do the interpretation, analysis, and conclusion steps if we don't know where our information came from. So you have to say how you know what you know. How you know is as important as what you know. So start now, while you're a beginner to genealogy, and carefully note where you get each piece of information. Do this as you find data.

When you begin your research by talking with family members, make notes about who you talked with. Record the date and place and your relationship to that family member. As you enter

Sample Research Report

Research Report on Andrew Collet (1784–1863) ——————— Family name
Was He a Son to Isaac Collet of Green County, Tennessee? ——————— Topic of the
report

Date: 5 January 2012 ——————————————————— Date your
report

Prepared by:
Gene E. Alogist
1956 Anystreet
Anytown, OH 12345 ——————————————————— Researcher's
name and
address

Proof exists that the records of Andrew Collet in Greene and Campbell Counties, Tennessee, and Cole County, Missouri, are all the same man. The argument for including Andrew as a son to the Isaac Collet family hinges on two documents: the sale of the estate of Isaac Collet and a deed in Greene County in which James Pebley sells his land to Abraham Collet. The first establishes that Isaac Collet likely left an heir named Andrew; the second links Andrew Collet to both Abraham Collet and James Pebley, who had moved from Greene County to Campbell County. There are multiple reasons for the assumption that the Andrew Collet of Campbell County is the Andrew Collet of Cole County, Missouri.

A brief
summary of
the question

Was Andrew Collet of Cole County, Missouri, the same man earlier seen in Campbell County, Tennessee?

This researcher
has listed all the
small questions
she had to answer
before coming to
a conclusion—a
good way to stay
organized!

1. Andrew's 1850 and 1860 Census listings in Cole County, Missouri, assert birth in Tennessee about 1784. (1850, Cole County, p. 55; 1860 Cole County, p. 227)

2. Andrew purchased property in Cole County, Missouri, by 1838. (Ford, *History of Cole, Moniteau, Morgan, Benton, Miller, Maries and Osage Counties, Missouri*. [Easley, SC: Southern Historical Press, 1978], p. 213) No man of this name lived in Missouri in the 1830 Census; only one appeared in Missouri in the 1840 Census. (Cole County, page 71)

Evidence

3. Only one man named Andrew Collet was on the 1830 Census of Tennessee, in Campbell County, page 228. That man is not seen in Tennessee in the 1840 Census.

4. The identified children of Andrew who were living at the time of the 1850 Census all show Tennessee births: Isaac Collet, born about 1811; Sarah Collet Smith (wife of Ali Smith), born 1822.

5. Andrew's younger identified son, Anderson Collet, served in the Mexican War in a unit formed in Campbell County, Tennessee. (National Archives film series M629, roll 8, "Index to Compiled Service Records of Volunteer Soldiers Who Served During Indian Wars and Disturbances, 1815–58") He died in Cole County, Missouri, in 1845. (Cole Co., MO, Probate packet 113A-4; entered probate 14 October 1845)

Evidence

Number your
pages to keep
them together.

Page 1 of 2 ————————————————————

Family History Detective

Put your
name and the
date on each
page of your
report

Prepared by: Gene E. Alogist ———————————————— 5 January 2012

Was Andrew Collet of Campbell County, TN, the same seen earlier in Greene County, TN?

1. Never from 1810 through 1830 do two men named Andrew Collet appear anywhere in the state. A man of this name left records in Greene County through the tax records of 1818, then appeared in the records of Campbell County in 1820, after which time he never again appeared in records of Greene County.

Evidence ——— 2. There is a deed in Greene County made 17 December 1816 in which James Pebley, then of Campbell County, sells his Greene County property to Abraham Collet of Greene County. This deed was witnessed by Andrew and John Collet. The deed was not proven and recorded until 1825, at which time only John Collet appeared to prove the document. This suggests that Andrew Collet was no longer available in Greene County to swear the deed and also provides a definite link between these localities. (Greene County Deed Book

Source ——— 12, p. 321)

3. Andrew Collet was witness to the will made 17 August 1833 in Campbell County by neighbor Charles Bratcher, a name that earlier occurred in Greene County. (Campbell County Will Book 1, p. 303)

This ——— **Conclusion**

conclusion is
a summary
of the
evidence
and the
results of the
research.

Yes, Andrew Collet of Cole County, Missouri, is the same man found earlier in Campbell County, Tennessee, and even earlier in Greene County, Tennessee. In that locality only Isaac Collet is a potential father, for he is the only man of the correct name and anywhere near the correct age. Isaac's probate consists of the naming of an administrator (which Andrew is not), and the report of the sale of Isaac's worldly goods. At this estate sale, Andrew Collet is the most prominent purchaser. He also names his first son, "Isaac," and sustains numerous, long-running associations with other men claimed as sons to Isaac. Andrew Collet is a son to Isaac Collet of Greene County, Tennessee, even though Andrew is noticeably omitted from the Washington County, Tennessee, modern family history book.

This researcher ——— **For further study**

has listed
some ideas
for further
investigation.

Theopolis Miller also bought very heavily at the sale of Isaac Collet. He is the only man whose surname is not Collet who took a share of crops. It is certainly possible that the wife of Theopolis is either Isaac's widow or an older Collet daughter. Pursue it—this family could use some girlish influence!
Search the records of neighboring Jefferson County as well, for Isaac Collet sold land there not long before his death … might turn up new views.

Page 2 of 2

Figure 2-1, This sample research report was written by a genealogist seeking to identify the father of Andrew Collet. She wrote out a statement of the question, and listed evidence and cited documents that supported her conclusion.

When you begin your research by talking with family members, make notes about who you talked with. information in a genealogy software program, you can use your notes as sources.

Your first searches for information are likely to be on the Internet. Be sure to capture the URL, the universal resource locater. (They often begin with *http://*.) URLs are important in the event you want to return to a site. Sometimes you can't, but if you have the URL, you might use the Way Back Machine at <www.archive.org> to retrieve a defunct site. The date you looked at a source on the Internet is important because websites' data changes. Rather than making a paper copy of interesting Internet sources, it's easy to save a copy in your computer files.

If your source is a printed volume, gather all the elements about the book just as you did when you were writing a high school term paper: title, author, publisher, and the year and place of publication. Don't worry about the order of these elements; never mind where the commas and periods go. Just be sure to make a note about them on the photocopies or notes you take from the book. Add another item: a reminder to yourself about the library or archive where you found the book. Many genealogy books are printed in small press runs, and some future researcher may wonder where a copy of the book is located. (The reminder may be helpful to you, as well.)

Do the same thing for magazine, newsletter, newspaper, and journal articles. Record the author, article title, periodical name, volume and issue, and the date of publication.

Though more and more materials are digitized and available in electronic form, some information is still only available on microfilm. When you're using that medium, you should record the same kind of information as for other published sources, but you'll add the microfilm roll number and any other identifying information.

A source you use for information may never have been published. It may be a letter, diary, public record, gravestone, church record, or even an e-mail message. In general, say who wrote it, what it is, where it is now, and give enough information so someone unfamiliar with your research could find that document or object again. Add notes about the condition of the item, or any special circumstances that impact your evaluation and analysis of it.

Sometimes it's difficult to decide whether a source is published or not. In general, if copies of it have been distributed, especially for commercial purposes, it's a published record. Web pages posted on the Internet are published records—they're there for public consumption.

A simple guide for basic source citation is included in the back of this book. The examples show you the elements of information you need to write a citation for many of the common kinds of documents genealogists use as evidence.

You may hear the argument from time to time that keeping up with sources is too time-consuming and too much trouble. It isn't *fun*, like finding new information about your ancestors. Without that source information, however, you can't evaluate what you've found. You can't analyze the information and draw conclusions. And you can't pass on what you've learned, because the cousin to whom you pass along your information is going to ask, "But how do you *know*?"

Come on, Sherlock, gather your toolbox of skills, and get ready to begin. Let's learn where to start your genealogical research in Step 3, Beginning at the Beginning.

KEY CLUES

- Question the validity of the sources you uncover.
- Take thorough notes and write summaries of your research results.
- Follow a consistent style for recording dates, number formats, and name conventions.
- Research your ancestors' extended family, neighbors, and friends to increase your success rate and climb further up your family tree.
- Focus your research on linking one generation at a time.
- Write research reports to clarify your thoughts, record your progress, and leave a record on where and how to continue future research.

BEGINNING AT THE BEGINNING
Your Family History Starts With You

Start your genealogy project with yourself. After all, when you started reading this book, you looked in the mirror, didn't you? (Because you wondered where you got those eyes.)

PROVE WHO YOU ARE

Your genealogical research starts with you. Begin by examining your birth certificate. You'll probably be surprised at the amount of information it contains. Depending upon the place and time period it was issued, it probably lists:

• your full name at birth
• your sex and whether or not you were part of a multiple birth
• date of birth
• county and state of birth
• usual residence of your mother
• mother's full maiden name
• her age and race
• state or foreign country of her birth

- number of her previous children
- number of her living children
- father's full name
- his age and race
- state or foreign country of his birth
- his usual occupation
- kind of business or industry in which he works
- name of the informant
- attending physician or midwife's name
- signature of the doctor or midwife
- name of the hospital or institution
- date of registration
- registration numbers of the certificate
- and usually the certification by the state registrar attesting
  that it is a true and correct copy of the record

If you don't already have a copy of your birth certificate, you can request one from the state bureau of vital records in the state where you were born. You've probably had to produce this document at some other time in your life—when you entered school, applied for a Social Security card, or had some other reason to prove who you are.

If your parents are alive, question them about the circumstances of your birth. Where did your family live when you were born? Is the house still there? Have you been back to visit? If your parents are deceased, perhaps you can question an older brother or sister, or one of your aunts or uncles.

School records may supply information about you. Not only the course of study, but family information is probably listed in them as well. You may remember the names of the schools you attended. Write to them and request copies of your records. If the school no longer exists, the state department of education may help you learn what happened to the records.

> When you begin your search for information about yourself, look for scrapbooks and photo albums.

If you're a member of a religious group, there are probably records in their files that contain personal information about you, and if you've been a member since childhood, the names of your parents may be a part of their records.

When you begin your search for information about yourself, look for scrapbooks and photo albums. Perhaps your parents kept a baby book for you with copies of your birth announcement and newspaper clippings about your birth.

If you're adopted, you have two sets of parents, one who chose you, the other biological. You're a part of your adoptive family, so you can research those family lines, as well as those of your natural

Figure 3-1, sample birth certificate: Your birth certificate is the perfect place to start your genealogy research. It contains a wealth of information.

The sources mentioned in this chapter are about documenting your life, but they'll apply, too, when you begin researching your relatives.

parents. Because of the secrecy usually involved in an adoption, it's frequently difficult to determine the identities of the natural parents. And because there was a break in the handing down of family traditions, adopted people sometimes face a tough research situation. A good overview of adoption research is Maureen Taylor's "All About Adoption Research" article available on Genealogy.com, at <www.genealogy.com/69_taylor.html>. Use your favorite Internet search engine to learn more about the adoption laws in effect at the time and place you were born. The situation isn't hopeless; it just takes more work and some time to learn about adoption research. *The Adoption Searchbook: Techniques for Tracing People* by Mary Jo Rillera is an example of the kind of book that can help with adoption research.

Make a list of the places you lived as a child. Try to remember the street addresses. If you can't remember the exact dates of moves your family made, correlate them with your school experience. Did you move between fifth and sixth grade? Ask older brothers and sisters for help.

Can you compile a list of all the jobs you've had? Construct a list just as though were you composing a résumé.

The Social Security Administration can supply you with a copy of form SS-5, the form you filled out to request your Social Security card. The SS-5 asked for information about you and your parents, including your mother's maiden name and the birthplaces of your parents. How much did you know then? You may be surprised about what you wrote on the form. Go to <http://ssa-custhelp.ssa.gov/app/answers/detail/a_id/321> to learn more about requesting your form. Or order online at <https://secure.ssa.gov/apps9/eFOIA-FEWeb/internet/main.jsp>.

Look at the amount of information that exists to document your life. See how much information is available about you? The sources mentioned in this chapter are about documenting your life, but they'll apply, too, when you begin researching your relatives.

By keeping what's important and winnowing your files, you'll make it easier for some genealogist in the future to learn about you.

Organize all this information, keeping the important papers and discarding only those that you know are not important. If you have doubts about whether to keep or toss an item, keep it. (Yes, it is difficult for anyone with a genealogical tendency to throw away records.) By keeping what's important and winnowing your files, you'll make it easier for some genealogist in the future to learn about you.

Organization is easier for most people if you scan your documents and save the files on your computer. Be careful; if you post sensitive personal information on your computer, you need to take precautions about security. Some versions of Microsoft Windows have Bit Locker, an encryption program, built in. And many vendors offer excellent software for this purpose.

WRITE ABOUT YOURSELF

Gather all the information you've found about yourself and consider writing your autobiography. Record your life story so your descendants can learn more about you when they begin their search for ancestors. Writing about your life will cause you to reflect upon it. Think of it as a prelude to your journal about your genealogical quest. For more information about writing your life story, see *My Life & Times* by Sunny Morton.

Encourage young people in your life to start a lifelong habit of journaling. Set aside family time to share excerpts, respecting privacy of course.

If you aren't quite ready for the autobiography project, begin writing in small segments about interesting events in your life. Keep a journal. You can keep a journal of your day-to-day life. Facebook and blogs offer journaling possibilities. Write about the little things. Record your thoughts and feelings. Keep writing, and someday you'll have some raw material for your autobiography. The journal itself will have value to your descendants.

Keep the journal in whatever format is easiest for you. If you want to handwrite it, why not buy a lovely blank book to inspire your thoughts? Maybe loose-leaf is a better idea if you write, then rewrite. If you're accustomed to typing your thoughts, keep an electronic journal. But do take time to store hard-copy, paper printouts of your journal. If your journal is created online, remember to create and maintain backup copies.

Keeping a journal can lift your spirits. When something especially wonderful happens, write about it and capture your feelings. Reread your journal entries from time to time, especially the uplifting parts.

Your search for your ancestors is like starting on a journey of discovery. Why not keep a journal about your experiences in finding your roots? Record more than just the places you went to do research and what you found. Express how you felt when you first found your grandparents on a federal census schedule, or learned the names of grandparents you didn't know before you started. Describe the faces of those new cousins you met through a common interest in genealogy. Do they look like you?

Genealogy research isn't just about your ancestors—it's about you, too. The journey of discovery isn't just about finding ancestors, it's about finding out who you are.

After you've found records about yourself, it's time to expand your research into home and family sources about your parents.

KEY CLUES

- Examine your birth certificate to learn details about your parents.
- If you don't have a copy of your birth certificate, request one from the state bureau of vital records in the state where you were born.
- Record the names of all the schools you attended and request transcripts from them.
- Check the records of religious groups you participated in for details about your involvement.
- Record the places where you lived as a child (including street address) along with the dates you lived there.
- List all of the jobs you've worked.
- Request a copy of your SS-5 form from the Social Security Administration.
- Start a journal to record everyday life.

RAIDING THE REFRIGERATOR
Searching Home Sources for Information

I t's time to remember the family stories, pull out the family photos, and gather the family papers that have been sitting around for years, waiting for someone to discover them. Your genealogical search begins at home. You started by gathering information about yourself and your life. Now it's time to expand your search and find information about your family members.

FAMILY STORIES

Family stories can be a wonderful part of your family history. Most families have some family legends that have been handed down. Most are verbal tales, no one ever wrote them on paper. It's difficult to recall all the stories you've heard. Some of the details are sure to escape you. When you think of a family tale, write out as much of it as possible. If you're not sure if you're remembering something correctly, include what you do remember and note your doubts.

Perhaps you heard family stories when you were a child. Grandpa may have told tales about his grandfather riding with the Jesse James outlaw gang. There may be a family story about the immigrant ancestor who left the "old" country to make a new life in America. Perhaps your grandmother remembers moving to California during the Great Depression of the 1930s.

Write the stories now! Put them on paper before they fade away. Family legends have a way of changing through time as they're told and retold. Everyone remembers them a bit differently. Seek out your older relatives and ask for their versions of the family stories. Don't add their versions to yours, write them separately and be sure to make a notation about who told you, and when and where you heard it.

Consider making an audio or video recording of your relatives telling family stories. Save the digital files on your computer. Ask older relatives about any bits of family information they remember. When did Uncle Charlie die? Was it before or after Cousin Clyde left for the Korean War? Ask about places, too. Where was Uncle Charlie buried?

Place names are very important in genealogy because public records are kept according to jurisdiction, which is usually based on geographic areas. Any clues your living relatives can supply about previous places of residence for family members will help you when your research turns to public records.

When you ask family members for information, they can't always supply exact dates, but they can often bracket the event. If Uncle Charlie died before Cousin Clyde left for the Korean War, was it before or after great-grandmother's death in 1947? If the family member remembers great-grandma being at Uncle Charlie's funeral, it was before 1947. Be careful, though. One researcher learned her ancestor died during "the year of the big flood." The river was too high for some members of the family to attend the funeral, her cousin remembered. Much has been written about the Flood of 1927, but a search for a newspaper obituary was fruitless. With more questions, she learned there was also a "big flood" in 1923. And that, the newspapers confirmed, was the year the ancestor died.

The best way to learn about interviewing techniques is to actually interview your relatives. Practice on close family members who'll forgive you for fumbling with the audio or video recorder and asking dumb questions. If you are unsure of what to ask, start with the questions from *Family Tree Magazine*'s article "20 Questions for Interviewing Relatives," <www.familytreemagazine.com/article/20-questions>. Sometimes, for the relatives you're around frequently, you don't need to conduct formal interviews to gather information—just be alert for clues about the past in your conversations.

In an interview, you're trying to learn your subject's story. It isn't a criminal interrogation or a legal deposition. Ask permission, then set up the interview for a specific place and time. Give your interviewee some advance notice about what you want to know. If you have them, you can take along photos, heirlooms, or documents to jump start the person's memory.

Don't tire your subject, and be sure you aren't doing all the talking. If you just ask for a series of names, dates, and places, you'll wear out your welcome in a hurry. Could you answer a series of rapid-fire questions about all the events in your life? It's better to ask leading, open-ended questions and gently guide the conversation toward your research objective.

People's memories operate in a strange way. There's a gap sometimes, especially for older folks, between the time the question is asked and when the answer pops up in their brains. That gap is

Don't put off

interviewing older relatives.

They may not be around when

you find time to visit.

sometimes a week or ten days. You'll be amazed if you return after that interval and ask your questions again. Those memories and the answers to your questions may have surfaced.

Don't put off interviewing older relatives. They may not be around when you find time to visit. Go back. After you've talked with your relatives, go and do some research in census and courthouse records. Take your new findings and revisit those relatives and ask for more details. A researcher had talked with relatives about her great-grandfather. They'd told her what a lovely person he'd been; such a kind and considerate old soul, they said. His newspaper obituary echoed those sentiments. But when she visited the courthouse, she found records showing her great-grandfather had paid several fines for "breach of the peace." When she asked the relatives for more information, they told her that the old boy had relived the Civil War on more than one occasion with a neighbor who'd fought on the other side.

VISITING FAMILY CEMETERIES

Older family members often make frequent trips to cemeteries where family members are buried. In rural areas, "cemetery working days" are popular. People with relatives buried in a particular country cemetery gather on an appointed day, often in the spring, and clean up the graveyard. They bring rakes and weed-eaters and a potluck lunch. It's an ideal time to meet distant cousins and gather genealogy information. Remember to take a rake to the event in addition to your notepad, so you'll blend in.

Depending upon the kind of cemetery where your relatives are buried there may or may not be information available. In some very remote, rural cemeteries the stones may have fallen over and the cemetery may have virtually disappeared. No one in the area may remember who the graves belong to, and no records may exist about the burials.

Many families established burial grounds on their own family farms. They may be located far from roads. If the farm or land isn't still currently owned by the family, the burial ground may have fallen into neglect. Though most all states have laws that allow access to cemeteries, even those on private property, it isn't a good idea to visit those cemeteries without permission from the landowner in the area.

Visiting remote cemeteries can be dangerous. When your great-aunt reminded you it was bad luck to walk on someone's grave, she was actually suggesting it could be downright dangerous. The ground could give way under your weight. A plain wooden coffin buried for two hundred years may have rotted away, leaving a potential sinkhole. Never go alone to remote areas. Plan your visit for a time of year that isn't hunting season. Search the Internet for hunting regulations in the state you're interested in. Genealogists know the best time of year to visit cemeteries that aren't well-maintained is in the dead of winter when vegetation and crawling critters are at a low ebb, unless of course the cemetery is knee-deep in snow.

Cemetery names change. The newspaper obituary you found from eighty years ago may say an ancestor was buried in "Pickens Cemetery." You search in vain for a cemetery by that name, only to have someone tell you it's known today as "Hawkins Cemetery" because the Hawkins family burials outnumber everyone else. Or you find "Mt. Zion" cemetery, which is mentioned on a death certificate, and don't find the gravestone for your ancestor in that cemetery. You learn later there is an "Old Mt. Zion" and a "New Mt. Zion." You, of course, searched the wrong cemetery.

There are lots of websites devoted to cemetery inventories. Many include photos of tombstones. A note of caution, however: Remember that because a particular cemetery or tombstone isn't mentioned on the Internet doesn't mean it doesn't exist. An older inventory preserved on microfilm or in book form in a library may list information from stones that are no longer in existence.

Think about your ancestor's life when you begin a search for the burial place. If, for example, your ancestor was Jewish, he may not be buried in a local cemetery; he may have been buried in a nearby city in a Jewish cemetery. If your ancestor died away from home, her body may have been transported home for burial. Or your ailing ancestor who went to a health spa may have died in that place and the burial may have taken place nearby. The city of Hot Springs, Arkansas, has people from all over the world buried in its cemeteries because the mineral baths were thought to be a cure for serious illnesses. People went there and died, and were buried in area cemeteries. If your ancestor was a veteran and died after the Civil War, he may have been buried in a national cemetery maintained by the federal government.

If the cemetery where your family members are buried is connected to a church, there may be records about the burials among the church's records. Through the mid-twentieth century, churches often had adjacent burial grounds. After World War II, however, large commercially run cemeteries began to replace family graveyards and church plots. Many cities maintain public cemeteries. If your family members are buried in large, well-maintained perpetual-care cemeteries, an employee may be able to supply detailed information not only about the burials, but also about who purchased the lots. City cemeteries usually have records about the burials there.

Whatever kind of cemetery you find, pay attention to the people buried near your relatives—they may be family members, too. A researcher noticed an unfamiliar name on a grave marker in the family plot. Further research showed the mystery marker belonged to the ancestor's mother-in-law, and opened a whole new family line.

SIFTING THROUGH FAMILY PAPERS

Look through family papers for income tax returns, bank statements, insurance policies, voter registration, military discharges, deeds and mortgages, and any records that might give you addresses and places of residence, and possibly Social Security numbers for family members. You'll find some families kept an abundance of family papers, others kept little. Some families were prolific letter writers; others left no written records.

Whatever amount of family records are available, go through them carefully. Make photocopies or scan all of the papers that might potentially be of use to your search. And write on the copies or in the metadata area of the computer files the name of the person from whom you received the material. (You knew, didn't you, that you can add comments and other information to your scanned image files? In your version of Windows, go to Help and Support and enter "change properties for a file." Add your comments in the properties dialogue box. Be sure to save the changes after you make them. Those comments and keywords you enter make searching for files much easier.)

Try to build a chronology of all the places you've lived since your birth. Then do the same for your parents. Remember to note your sources for the facts you find. Location, location, location—it's important in genealogy, too.

If you find family papers in the possession of your parents and grandparents with names on them you don't recognize, be aware those names may have significance later as your research progresses. Look, too,

Figure 4-1, Enlightenment by Journal: While cleaning the garage in preparation for a move, one genealogist found her father's journal tucked into one of his old college textbooks. The journal was apparently an assignment for a class and had lain in a trunk undisturbed since the 1930s. As you can see from the entry reproduced here, documents like this can lend remarkable insight into the lives and personalities of our ancestors.

When I entered junior high my size brought me in contact with the game of football. Although I was big for my age, I was a poor football player because it seems that I had trouble moving very fast. With my athletic career at a low ebb my thoughts turned to love. It was the real thing; although I wouldn't admit it ever to the young lady. It got so I would thrill at the mere sight of her, but this all ended when I saw her with another fellow. With that I felt as if I were a social out-cast and was ready to end it all. Some how I was able to regain my social standing, only to have it drop to a lower ebb. This happened during our graduation exercises. When my name was called to go up on the stage and receive my diploma, I missed the first step and fell flat on my face.

at the spelling of names in the documents. Your family names may have been spelled differently by various clerks who created the documents you uncover.

When you begin your search in family papers, look for copies of vital record certificates—birth and death certificates—among your family records. A death certificate should contain the name of the cemetery where the deceased person was buried. A death certificate for one of your aunts or uncles may lead you to a family cemetery where your great-grandparents, who died before deaths were recorded on a statewide basis, are buried.

Frequently, family cemeteries are far removed from your present residence. You may not be able to go to the family cemetery, but someone may have compiled a published inventory. We'll talk more about finding that sort of resource in the chapter on visiting libraries and archives.

STUDY FAMILY PHOTOGRAPHS

Study family photos. Identifying information written on the backs may offer clues to relationships. "Your aunt, Bertha Barham," was written on the back of a photo in a researcher's collection. She didn't know who Bertha was, or whose aunt she'd been, but since the photo was among those preserved by the family, she knew Bertha must be a relative. Eventually, she discovered her great-grandmother had a sister Bertha. Further research turned up a marriage for that Bertha to a Mr. Barham. When Bertha's descendants were located, they were delighted to receive a copy of the photo. And they were able to share Bertha's parents' family Bible with the researcher.

Look for photographers' logos on photos that might tell you a place name. Search the Internet for the photographer. One photograph of two young boys had nothing written on the back about their identities, but the photographer's mark on the border of the photo said, "Purcell, I.T." (I.T. was a commonly used abbreviation for "Indian Territory," an area that became eastern Oklahoma after statehood in 1907.) A check of records in that place revealed information about a lost branch of the family. Previously unknown family members there recognized the boys in the photo. Their branch of the family had preserved letters received in the late nineteenth century from the researcher's family members.

To learn more about using photos in your family history research, go to the Photo Detective blog, <blog.familytreemagazine.com/photodetectiveblog>. Read *Uncovering Your Ancestry Through Family Photographs* by Maureen A. Taylor.

LOCATING VITAL RECORDS

A favorite place to record family vital information in previous years was the family Bible. If you're lucky enough to locate one for your family, photograph the family record pages and the title page of the Bible. Take several photos of each page in natural light, some of the entire page, and others zoomed in. Prop your elbow on something to steady the camera if you need to. Photograph the owner holding the Bible. If you aren't able to photograph the Bible, you may have to transcribe the information from it, but a photograph is much better. Check for loose papers inserted in the Bible—you may find newspaper obituary clippings or funeral memorial cards. Don't remove them from their original place—they may mark favorite or meaningful Bible passages—just photograph them in place. Be sure to make notes about who has the Bible now and who the former owners of the Bible were. You may find some family members very possessive about their ownership of a family Bible. Assure them you just want the information, and offer to share future research results with them.

After you've talked with relatives, searched through the family papers you can locate, and visited family cemeteries, it's time to order copies of vital records. Go to the government's Center for

Before you request a certificate, check information about the dates when the various states began keeping birth and death records on a statewide basis.

Disease Control website, <cdc.gov/nchs/w2w.htm>, to learn about each state's vital records office. (For births and deaths in foreign countries, do an Internet search to find the national site, then follow the links to smaller political entities.) Before you request a certificate, check information about the dates when the various states began keeping birth and death records on a statewide basis. If, for example, your grandmother died in Arkansas in 1911, there's no need to order a search of the death records, because Arkansas didn't begin keeping statewide death records until February, 1914. But if that same grandmother had died in Missouri, there might be a certificate on file for her, as Missouri's consistent, statewide death records begin in 1910.

After you've learned whether statewide vital records were kept in the particular state you're interested in for the time period when your ancestors were born or died, check to see if indexes to the records you need are available online. In some states, like Missouri, images of the documents themselves are posted online. Order copies if the images aren't available online.

Just because there should be a state vital record doesn't mean there will be. Compliance with the laws requiring registration of births and deaths wasn't universal in the early years. The event may never have been reported. Or the record may have been lost. Or the record may be there, but the name is misspelled either on the original or in the index and it can't be located. Vital records can potentially be very rewarding, so it's worth the effort.

Armed with the vital records you've ordered and all the other family information you've gathered, it's time to organize your materials before you delve into research in libraries and archives.

PRIVACY LAWS

When you begin your genealogical research, begin with yourself. Public records about you are available to you because you have a right to that information. When you begin making inquiries about other people, even though they're related to you, you must consider privacy laws.

You wouldn't want personal information about yourself available to just anyone, would you? Much of it is already public record. In most counties, marriage and divorce records are open to any researcher. But those same records at the state level may be restricted by privacy laws. Some states restrict access, even at the county level, to records less than fifty years old. The custodian of the records you're interested in will be familiar with the restrictions on the records in that jurisdiction.

Do you remember when the federal census was last taken? You were required by law to fill out the forms or otherwise answer the questions, but you were assured the information would be kept private. And it is kept private for seventy-two years. You can obtain copies of information from unreleased census records about yourself from the Personal Service Branch, Bureau of the Census, PO Box 1545, Jeffersonville, IN 47131. Form BC-600 describes fees and requirements and is available online at <census.gov/genealogy/www/bc-600.pdf>. Some people who do not have birth certificates on file use this unreleased census information as proof of age to support an application for a delayed birth certificate.

The Social Security Administration will furnish information about deceased people to anyone, regardless of relationship. Deceased people have no privacy rights, according to federal policies. But you may have to prove the person you're inquiring about is dead. Social Security maintains a database of deceased folks who had Social Security numbers, most of whom died after 1964 when the agency began computerizing their records. There are several online sources for this free information. One of them is <ssdi.rootsweb.ancestry.com>. If you find someone of interest, you can order a copy of Form SS-5, the form filled out by a person to obtain a Social Security card, at <https://secure. ssa.gov/apps9/eFOIA-FEWeb/internet/main.jsp>.

Military service records for people who served in the armed forces in the last seventy-five years are protected by privacy laws. Most of these records are housed at the National Personnel Records Center, 9700 Page Blvd., St. Louis, MO 63132. However, under the 1974 Freedom of Information Law, some data from the records can be released to people other than the serviceperson. Read more about it here: <archives.gov/st-louis>.

Release of information in private records is up to the record-holder. Funeral homes, for example, are private, commercial concerns. They usually furnish information to genealogists about people for whom they've conducted services, but they're under no obligation to do so. Hospitals are very careful about releasing any information that would violate a person's privacy.

Most privacy laws allow you to request information about a living person if that person signs a release. You've encountered this when your insurance company asks you to sign a release so medical information about you from a doctor or hospital can be sent to the company.

It's frustrating to have your research reach a stopping point because of privacy laws, but remember that your privacy is protected as well.

After you gathered all the records about your family that are available to you, it's time to organize the material and assess your information so you'll know where to begin your search in libraries and archives.

KEY CLUES

- Collect family memories and conduct interviews before it's too late.
- Consider making an audio or video recording of your relatives telling family stories.
- Investigate people buried near your relatives. They may be family members, too.
- Build a chronology of all the places an ancestor has lived since birth.

A PLACE FOR EVERYTHING
Keeping Records

If you don't start organizing your genealogical materials as you collect them, you're going to get very confused somewhere down the road. If you've already started collecting materials, it's time to put them into some kind of order before you get discouraged about the amount of time it takes you to find a particular piece of information in your records.

On the other hand, you can get so bogged down in organizing papers that you lose sight of your objective and don't have time to do actual research. So strike a balance between chaos and obsessive neatness. Think about the person who might find your genealogy research notes when you're no longer available—will your organizational system be self-evident? Can that person pick up your work and continue? Even more important, if you lay your genealogy aside for a few years, can you come back to it and retrieve your train of thought?

Computers make wonderful organizational tools and there are dozens of fine software programs on the market for managing a genealogical database. Programs today let you attach scanned photographs, documents, and audio and video clips to data. When you reach the stage of writing about your family's history, computer programs will greatly simplify your task.

How do you select genealogy software? Talk to friends and family who've already selected a program. Use an Internet search engine to find "genealogy software reviews." The program most widely used at this writing is Ancestry's Family Tree Maker (FTM). It's an excellent program, but so are several others. Go to <familytreemaker.com> to learn more about it. FTM is available for both Windows and Mac operating systems.

Genealogy software is also available to use online in what's called "cloud" computing. The advantage is that your files are available wherever you can lay your fingers on a keyboard connected to the Internet. The disadvantages, of course, are that your files are only available while there's an Internet connection, and if something goes amiss with the software company you've chosen, your files may not be safe. Ancestry.com offers a cloud computing option now—you can create, manage, and store your family tree online at their site.

Family Tree Maker is integrated with Ancestry.com's amazing collection of genealogy resources and databases. Once you begin entering your family's information, you can let the software compare your records with Ancestry.com's data and lead you to fresh information and new cousins who are working on your family lines. Though Ancestry.com has some free features, the bulk of its information is available through paid subscriptions. Source citations are automatically included when you add information to your Family Tree Maker files from Ancestry.com. The latest version of Family Tree Maker will even help you write a family history and publish your story.

In the "good old days," we used to develop paper filing systems for family group sheets and pedigree charts. It was like digging ditches without a backhoe—entirely possible but painfully slow. Paper family group sheets are still useful as worksheets, especially when you're interviewing relatives. Pedigree charts are useful in the same way. But when it comes to organizing all your information, it's difficult to imagine doing it without a computer. However, even with a computer, the tasks of analyzing and evaluating the information you discover are still up to you. To get you started and tide you over until you can make a genealogy software decision, we've included traditional paper forms in the appendix to this book.

CREATING FAMILY GROUP SHEETS

Start your organizational system around nuclear families—one set of parents and their children. Begin with yourself. If you're a married person, make a family group sheet for yourself and your spouse and your children, if you have any. Use the preprinted forms found in the appendix of this book or simply start adding information to your genealogy software. Either way, be sure to make notes about your sources as you record the data. Put those notes on the back of the paper group sheet, using the source guide in the back of this book to tell you what data elements to record about each source. Number your source list. Use those numbers you've assigned to your sources to indicate exactly what pieces of information on your group sheet came from each source. You won't need the numbers when you enter your sources in your genealogy software—it takes care of footnotes for you.

For example, if you use your birth certificate as the source of information about your date and place of birth and your parents' names, then your source notation might read something like this, "State of Ohio Birth Certificate #9-87654-321 for Terry Smith." If you've listed that item as source number two on your family group sheet, then place a "2" beside each data item supported by the birth certificate. If information is supplied verbally by a relative, write the person's name, address, and the date you heard the information. If you're writing in your marriage date or the births of your children, you might list yourself as the source, because you were present for the events. Of course, you were present at your birth, too, but you weren't a very reliable witness at the time.

In Family Tree Maker, you create a master source list and link pieces of data to it. It's easy and straightforward. Then when you generate family group sheets and other reports, your sources will appear on them.

Be consistent about the way you write dates (see the discussion in Chapter 2). Most genealogists write dates with the day of the month first, then the month spelled out as a word, followed by the year as a four-digit number. Thus, 25 July 1950. Also be consistent about the way you write place names. Write the city, town, or village name first, then the county, followed by the state, for places within the United States. For foreign countries, use the same format—local name, province, country. If you using Family Tree Maker, the software will help you keep your data entry consistent.

After you've filled out a family group sheet for your family, either on paper or in your computer software, complete one with your parents and list yourself as one of the children on the form. Then complete group sheets for your mother's parents and your father's parents. The method is the same whether you're using a paper form or a form presented on your computer monitor from a software program.

You may find one paper group sheet doesn't supply enough room for all your sources or all the children of a particular couple. Simply write "continued on page 2" in the bottom margin and note "continued from previous page," on the top of the second sheet. You need not repeat all the details about the couple, just re-enter their names at the top of the second page. Your genealogy program will take care of this for you when it generates a report from your data.

You should fill out group sheets for each marriage or relationship that resulted in children. If you're using a computer program, it will automatically generate a group sheet for each married couple. Some people will be listed on more than one group sheet. If your grandmother was married three times and had children by all three of her husbands, there should be three separate sheets for her, one with each husband, listing just the children from that union. If you're using paper group sheets, note cross-references on each sheet to help you remember there were other marriages. Don't just make a group sheet for the couple from whom you're descended—you'll omit some of your cousins from your family history. Remember—one group sheet per marriage. In your genealogy software, use the function to add a spouse in the case of multiple marriages.

What if you don't know the name of both parents? Enter as much information as you know. One thing for certain, there were two parents. You might encounter "non-paternal events," that is, a child born from two people who weren't married. At least not married to each other. You may learn about a child whose natural or biological father isn't the father on the birth certificate. What do you do? First, consider the feelings of living people involved. As long as the information remains private in your records, you can write whatever you want, but when you decide to publish it, you've opened a new set of questions. Each situation is different, but omitting information is better than hurting someone's feelings.

Put your name and address on each paper group sheet. If you leave one you're working on at the library, it can find its way home. If you share one with other genealogists, they'll know who created it. Family Tree Maker lets you enter your "user information" one time, then prints it on all your reports automatically.

Again, keeping genealogical records without computer software designed especially to manage them is possible. But as you begin to accumulate more and more family group sheets, you'll see the value of computerizing those records. Choose software and begin! If you find a better choice later, the GEDCOM standard, a file specification for exchanging information between programs, will let you transfer the information you've entered to another program.

CONSTRUCTING PEDIGREE CHARTS

You can mentally organize your ancestors for the first two or three recent generations. After that, your family tree may resemble a thicket instead of single tree, if you don't create a pedigree chart to help you visualize your direct lineage. Unlike group sheets, pedigree charts only show your direct ancestors. Grandfather's brothers and sisters are included on a family group sheet for your great-grandparents, but only your grandparents and their parents (and their parents and so on) are listed on a pedigree chart.

If you're using a computer program, you can automatically generate a pedigree chart from the data you've entered. With a paper system, you'll have to fill out a pedigree chart, using the information on your group sheets. You'll use pedigree charts to share your lineage information with other researchers. Pedigree charts are available in a variety of styles and sizes and a sample chart is available in the appendix.

People on your pedigree chart are numbered in a particular way. You're number one. (You *knew* that!) Your father is number two on the chart; your mother is number three. Your father's father is number four; your father's mother is number five; your mother's father is number six; and her mother's mother is number seven. You'll notice a pattern developing here. Except for number one (that's you), all the men on the chart have even numbers, and all the women have odd numbers. Any person on the chart's father's number is twice their number. Thus, your mother's father's number is six, twice that of your mother's number which is three. Your mother's father's father's number is twelve. A wife's number is always one more than her husband's number. Your father's lines are called your "paternal" lines and occupy the top half of your pedigree chart; your mother's are your "maternal" lines, and occupy the bottom half.

One kind of printout you can request from most genealogy computer programs is an "ancestor chart," also sometimes called an "*ahnentafel* chart." These charts use the same numbering system found on pedigree charts though the presentation of the information is a bit different.

Filling out family group sheets and pedigree charts can help you mentally organize your information. They're graphic representations of the data you've collected. Remember when you were in school and you heard teachers' lectures? You probably remembered more if you took notes. But if you used the information and made a diagram or chart from it, then you really learned it. It's the same with group sheets and pedigree charts, even though there's not going to be a quiz over who your ancestors were.

NOTE TAKING

You'll find yourself taking notes as you talk to people and study materials about your family. As soon as you find yourself writing information about your family, start making an effort at consistent, systematic note keeping. For handwritten notes, try to use standard, letter-size paper. Avoid the backs of envelopes and tiny scratch pads—they're hard to keep up with as they can be mistaken for trash or fall out of folders.

If you plan to keep your notes (and therefore file them later), write about only one family per piece of paper. That way, it'll be obvious where to file it when the time comes. At the top of the page, make it standard practice to write the family name involved, the current date, and details about your source—whether it's a person or a book. If it's a computer source, the best way to take notes is electronically. Open your word processor in a window and type your notes, including information cut-and-pasted from your online source. Be sure to note the URL as your source. Save your file. Windows 7 includes a nice feature that's helpful when you're capturing notes from your computer screen—it's called Snipping Tool and it's in your Accessories program folder (go to Start, All Programs, Accessories, Snipping Tool). Play with it to learn how to use it. Essentially you can capture almost anything that appears on your screen and copy it to the Windows Clipboard, then into a file of its own or into other software applications.

Avoid using metal clips and rubber bands in the materials you're going to keep in your paper files for a long time. Never use transparent tape of any kind. Metal clips will eventually rust and make ugly stains on the paper they touch. Use plastic or plastic-coated wire paper clips instead. Rubber bands turn into nasty things as they age. They're just innocent-looking rubber bands when you use them, but hidden in your files, they take on a new life and become sticky, gummy monsters. Swear off rubber bands. Transparent tape of any kind should never find a home in your papers. Like rubber bands, it looks helpful, then becomes a nightmare in a few years. It turns yellow and adhesive oozes out from its edges and damages and stains everything within reach. Eventually (after the damage) it dies and turns loose of the paper it was applied to.

Don't recopy your handwritten notes. Every time you transcribe or copy anything, you're introducing a possible new set of errors. You're also wasting time. Make your notes neat enough the first time to use without recopying. Verify what you've written. It only takes a few minutes to look back over what you've written and compare it with your source to ensure you didn't miscopy or leave out any important element.

Scan your handwritten notes and turn them into computer files. Enter information from your notes into your genealogy software. In Family Tree Maker, you can attach your files in the "Media Pane." You might make a notation on your handwritten notes when you've entered the information from them into your genealogy software—something like "entered FTM 4 July 2012."

If you're taking notes in a library or archival facility, first read the rules. Some archives require that you leave your coat, briefcase, and any other personal objects in a locker before using original manuscript materials. You may only be permitted to take in a single pencil and two sheets of notebook paper. Think positive: At least you're allowed to keep your clothes on, and the next time you want to use the materials, they'll be there. Some don't permit the use of cameras or portable scanners. Most allow use of personal computers, but if you don't take along your notebook computer, you may have to take notes the old-fashioned way.

When possible, photograph or photocopy the materials you need to take information from. Be sure to photocopy the title page of a book or periodical.

Sometimes, the time you have to spend in a library is limited. When possible, photograph or photocopy the materials you need to take information from. Be sure to photocopy the title page of a book or periodical and check to be sure it has all the elements you'll need to write a complete source citation. Note the repository, too. Genealogy books are often printed in very small press runs and you may wonder later where you found a particular book if you have to refer to it again. If you plan to reuse the book in that same library, note the call number in your notes or photograph the spine. The call number may be different in another library, but make a note of it, since it will save time in retrieving the book the next time you need to use it in that library. If you can't use your camera and must make photocopies, you can scan them later into computer files.

If you don't have a portable scanner or aren't permitted to use one, your digital camera is an ideal tool for note taking. Use the macro (close-up) setting to photograph everything from book pages to microfilm reader screens. Some smart phones have scanners and cameras that can help you take notes. Optical character recognition (OCR) software can render editable text from digital photo files. It's amazing!

A RESEARCH CALENDAR

A list of the sources you've searched is called by various names: research calendar, research log, source organizer, research index, or something else. Whatever you call it, a research calendar helps you keep track of the materials you've searched. It's essentially a list of sources you've examined.

You may need a research calendar for each surname you're working on. Or you may want to make one for each locality you're researching. Try the locality method first, and if it doesn't work out, change your method of keeping up with the sources you've searched to suit your research habits.

If, for example, you're working on Randolph County, North Carolina, you may have more than one family line that lived in that place. If you made research calendars for each surname, you'd have to write your entries on more than one calendar.

To create a research calendar, label a sheet of paper with the title you've assigned to it: "Randolph County, North Carolina, Research Calendar," for example. Be sure to put your name, address, and phone number on the page in the event you accidentally abandon it after a hard day at the library. Make ruled columns on the page and label them source, purpose, notes, date, and repository. Or simply use the form supplied in the appendix of this book.

When you visit the library (which we'll do in the next chapter of this book) and find a book that might contain information on your family, pull out your research calendar and make an entry for that source. List author, title, date and place of publication, and publisher. In the "purpose" column, write the surnames you're looking for. Note the date and repository, too.

The same routine applies to researching online sources as well. Note the URL and the date of your search. Databases and websites change, so the date is especially important for these sources.

If you didn't find anything of interest in the book or website, write "nothing located" or something like that in the "notes" column in your research calendar. Why list a book or website that didn't help you? Someday you might see that book's title in a bibliography or some other source and you might spend considerable time and effort locating that volume, just to be disappointed all over again. Or you might look at the date you searched a particular website and decide it's time to search it again for added information. If you make a note about your negative search on the first encounter, it may save you some time later. Then again, you might discover another family line in that same location. You can pull out your research calendar and see that you did search that title or URL but only for the Smith and Jones names, not the Abernathys. And you'd know you need to search again for the new surname.

If you do find something of interest in the source you've searched, you can write the relevant page numbers on your calendar. Or you might write, "see notes." Or note the name of a computer file you created from your notes. If the book isn't indexed and you only had time to scan the first three chapters, make a note of that, so you'll know where to pick up next time.

At first, when you check books and websites that look promising, you'll only look for the names you recognize as your family lines. After a while, you'll wise up and begin to check for all the names of associates of your family. Your research calendar will help you remember what sources you need to go back to.

Depending upon your personal preferences, you might set up your research log in a database or spreadsheet program, or you might keep it in Word. The most important aspect of keeping a research calendar is to create one that makes sense to you and maintain it.

Some people use their research calendars as a sort of master source list. They write an abbreviation for a particular source on their research notes. You may not want to follow that plan. There's

Figure 5–1, Research Calendar: Notice that this researcher not only wrote down what she found, but also what she didn't find. In the 1870 Census of Atchison County, Missouri, for instance, she found no listings for Ewing Murray or Sarah Robertson. By making a note of this, she will prevent herself from looking twice in the same place.

Research Calendar

Note the records you've checked for ancestral clues.

Researcher: *Bess Calhown*   Ancestor: *Ewing Murray*

Locality: *Atchison, MO & Cherokee KS*   Time Period: *1860+*

Brief Problem Statement: *Identify children of Ewing Murray & Sarah Robertson*

SEARCH DATE	WHERE AVAILABLE	CALL #	TITLE/AUTHOR/ PUBLISHER/YEAR OR RECORD IDENTIFICATION INFORMATION	NOTES	PAGE #s
12 May 2012	Courthouse Atchison, MO	——	Intestate probate packet of James Robertson 17 Nov 1879	Names "sister Sarah Murry of Cherokee Co., KS"	——
"	"	——	Atchison Co. Marriage Book A 1845–1863	No marriage for Ewing & Sarah	——
29 May 2012	Dallas Public Library		1860 Census of Atchison Co., MO	Children: Mary E 5, Jonathan 3, Emalisa 11/12	p. 525
"	"		1870 Census of Atchison Co., MO	Not there	

Note complete

source information on each

of your research notes pages, in

addition to writing the citation in

your research calendar.

no guarantee your research calendar will always be available to go with your notes. It's probably a better idea to note complete source information on each of your research notes pages, in addition to writing the citation in your research calendar.

When you move from published sources to original records, a research calendar is especially valuable. If you read the entire 1850 census on microfilm for Randolph County, North Carolina, note that on your calendar. If, on the other hand, you just looked at a printed index, make that distinction in your research calendar. Or if you used Ancestry.com's index, note that instead. And if you used a transcription instead of the census film itself, note that, too, along with the name of the person who made the transcription and other publication information.

Keeping a research calendar takes discipline. If you develop the habit at the beginning of your genealogical research career, it will seem second nature later on. And as you progress from a beginner to an advanced researcher, you'll earn respect from your peers who will appreciate your professional approach.

FILING DOCUMENTS

As you begin the process of filling out family group sheets, you'll see the need to organize the paper documents from which you took information. Start a filing system based on your group sheets; that is, label a file folder for each family for whom you've made a group sheet. This may sound a bit sexist, but label the folder with the husband's name first, then the wife's. Only in recent times and on a limited basis have wives kept their birth (maiden) names as their surnames. Women did, and frequently still do, assume the surnames of their husbands. This is also the way most genealogical collections are organized. Then again, creativity in your research is a good thing, so if you feel strongly about this subject, by all means, put the woman's name first and arrange your filing system that way—these are your files after all. Do be consistent, however.

Put the documents you've found, or copies of the documents, in the folder for the family they concern. Your grandparents' marriage license will go, for example, in the folder you've labeled with their names. The information from that license, along with a note about your source, will go on their family group sheet, either on paper or in your computer genealogy software.

If you're using a computer program, you might scan the important documents and store them as graphic images. Some genealogy software programs will allow you to establish links between data items and image files. Even if you scan the documents, you'll probably still want to store your originals in some order and the easiest way is to organize them by family groups.

File the folders alphabetically according to the husband's name (there's that sexist problem again) if that's the way you've set up your folders. You can start out with a box sized to accommodate standard file folders. Soon, you'll find yourself shopping for a file cabinet, then another. Genealogy is a paper-intensive business. But wait! There's a better way.

Instead of committing everything to paper, consider keeping electronic files to cut down on the papers you save (and file). There are some papers, especially old family documents and letters, and originals of vital records, you'll want to keep. Scanning those will cut down on handling them and they'll last longer. Your research notes are easily kept as computer files. Genealogy software manages data, eliminating the need to keep paper working copies after you've entered the information from them. If you go to a library to do research, you can print copies of group sheets for the families you're currently researching. Or just take your notebook computer along.

Electronic copies of your records are more easily backed up than a file cabinet full of paper files. All your genealogy data needs a routine backup plan. Online services, such as Mozy.com and Carbonite.com (and others), use your Internet connection to copy your files to their secure servers. You also need to create local backups to external hard drives. Digital storage media get smaller, faster, and cheaper. As new options become available—solid state drives are just now on the market—move your data to new media.

These family group sheets you've filled out or generated from computer information have another purpose. You'll find yourself contacting other researchers to ask for information. Don't be the person who says, "Send me everything you have on the Whatever family." (Substitute one of your family's surnames for "Whatever.") How will they know which materials you've already found? Instead, send a copy of your family group sheet on the family you have in common along with your pedigree chart so they can see how you're descended from their ancestor. If you've noted the sources you've used on the group sheet, your correspondent will have a list of the documents you've used, and will know which ones in their possession might be of most benefit to you. You can send that information electronically by printing a group sheet from your genealogy software. But instead of printing it on paper, print it to a PDF (Adobe's portable document format), a common file exchange type most computers on this planet can read. Attach the file to an e-mail.

ASKING FOR INFORMATION

As you move from searching sources in your home, you'll begin to correspond with people who can help with additional information. Some contacts will be one-time events—just an e-mail and a response. Others will be ongoing. You can file one-time correspondence, a request and reply about a marriage license for example, in the folder for the family it concerns. You might establish separate folders on your computer for the messages from your ongoing correspondents. To save e-mail messages, choose "file," then the "save-as" option in most any e-mail program. Saving e-mail as text (.txt) files ensures you can read messages later without compatibility issues.

Believe it or not, there are some folks out there who don't have computers or prefer to correspond with letters through the postal service. You can scan those into electronic files. Save copies of your letters to them, too.

Communication is one of the mainstays of genealogical research. After you've talked with all the living relatives you can locate and surveyed the sources you can find at home, it's time to start asking for information.

Yes, you can use the phone, but there are limits to phone conversations. People in the business world know the frustrations of playing "telephone tag," where you leave a message for someone and your call is returned, but you're away, so your answering machine or voice mail takes the message, so you can make another attempt later. Your call may come at an inconvenient time for the person you're calling. You'll have no record of the information you learn in a call—unless you take notes and that's distracting while you're talking.

There are times to use the phone. Your call to the reference desk of the local library is probably appropriate if it conforms to library policy. Calling a newly found cousin to chat (after you've e-mailed and asked about a convenient time to call) can be fun. Calling your grandmother on a regular basis is a good idea, too.

Before you send an e-mail to ask a question, check the Internet to be sure the answer isn't already posted somewhere. Spend a little time learning about how search engines work and you'll make better inquiries.

Most mail now is electronic and it's fast and simple. Some tips will make your e-mail correspondence more effective.

- **BE BRIEF.** Write a meaningful subject line.
- **BE CLEAR ABOUT WHAT YOU'RE ASKING FOR.** It's a good idea to have this notion worked out before you put your fingers on the keyboard.
- **ADD FULL CONTACT INFORMATION IN YOUR E-MAIL.** Use the "signature" function in your e-mail program to do this automatically.
- **BE NICE.** Remember your manners. Phrase your requests as just that—not demands. "Please" and "thank you" go a long way. Offer to pay for what you're requesting. Follow up with a thank-you note.

Direct your message to the correct person or agency. Do a little preliminary research. If you're asking for a marriage record, be sure it's directed to the right clerk's office in the correct courthouse.

Confine your message to one or two questions at most. Many repositories have a policy of only responding to one-question inquiries, and directing a list of professional researchers to the writers of multi-question letters. You can probably ask again if you have more questions.

Try to put all the information necessary (and no more) in the body of your e-mail. Some people and agencies have policies about not opening e-mail attachments.

For correspondents who've never met you, your letter is you to them. If it's poorly written with misspelled words and bad grammar, it makes a statement. A negative statement. And genealogical correspondence tends to hang around for years. Your message might end up in a manuscript collection one hundred years from now. Remember when your mother told you not to go out without wearing clean underwear in case you had a wreck? Well, don't send out a poorly presented message in case it should live on in some library's files.

Save your outgoing messages—the ones that end up in your "Sent" box. When you reply to an e-mail message, leave the conversation thread at the bottom of the message so it'll be easier to see what was said.

PHOTOGRAPHY

Scan old photos! Add them to your genealogy software—that's the Media Pane in Family Tree Maker. Scan resolution should be at least 300 dpi and more for small photos with fine details. Save them as TIF (tagged image file format) or JPG (Joint Photographic Expert Group) files. Give them descriptive file names.

Take your digital camera to every family event and shoot photos of everyone. Hand your camera to others to be sure you get in those photos, too. Keep your camera handy at home to record those special moments that pop up. Document heirlooms with photos. Photograph cemetery grave markers. Many cameras have the ability to attach a brief audio file to a photo—get out your camera manual and learn about that feature so you can read aloud the writing on a tombstone if it's difficult to photograph. If rules permit, use your camera in libraries and archives (without the flash, of course) to take notes. With the flash off and your elbow propped on the table to steady your camera, take photos of microfilm reader screens. Experiment! The results are right there instantly on your camera's monitor.

Start now and encourage your children to take photographs. Even a two-year-old grandchild can operate the camera in an iPhone. Taking well-composed, interesting photos is a learned skill and one of the best ways to learn is by doing. It's a creative endeavor and kids love those kinds of learning experiences.

Add comments about who, what, when, and where in each file's properties dialogue box. To learn how to do that, go to Windows Help and Support, then to "change the properties in a file." Use the comments field to annotate photos.

Save, save, save. Make backups of those photo files. Copy them to external desktop and portable hard drives. Copy them to photo storage sites online. Use an automated backup service to back up all your files and include your photo files in those backups.

Share copies of your photos with your relatives. Use online sites or e-mail to share photos, but order prints for non-computer users in your family. The more copies you distribute of your photos, both electronically and in print, the more likely they'll survive for future generations to enjoy.

Create photo books with your images to share with family and friends. There's more about this in the discussion about publishing your family history.

KEY CLUES

- Create a record-keeping system that is easy to maintain and helps you, or someone else, continue your research even after years of neglect.

BRANCHING OUT
Beginning Research Online and in Libraries and Archives

At some point in your genealogical quest, you're going to run out of material in the possession of your family members. And you're going to run out of living family members who can contribute information. Exhaust all those home sources and knowledgeable relatives first. Study and organize everything you find and are told. Analyze the information carefully. After you've done that, it's time to broaden your search to explore online databases and resources and then move into research at libraries and archives.

The first stage of your broadened search should include finding previously unknown cousins who are working on the same family lines you're interested in, and information about your family lines published in books or periodicals. The Internet makes it easy. The second stage of research involves finding original records and making your own analysis and evaluation of those materials.

The two stages actually overlap. You may have to do research in census and other original records to extend your information far enough back in time to connect to printed family histories. And after you discover new family lines, you'll need to search for more researchers and printed materials.

As you do research online and in libraries, remember to maintain a research calendar like the one described in a previous chapter.

STARTING YOUR SEARCH IN OUTSIDE SOURCES

Historians call the initial search for previously published books and articles on a subject, a "survey of the literature." You might call it prevention against reinventing the wheel. If some distant cousin has done diligent research and carefully constructed a pedigree, that work could save you years of finding all that information yourself. But just because you find something online or in print about your ancestors doesn't mean it's true. You'll still need to examine original records to verify what you read, but previously done research can be very helpful.

The Internet is like a giant candy store for genealogists. The amount of information available is overwhelming. It's difficult to recommend specific books about online genealogical resources because the material changes so rapidly. One of the most comprehensive collections of links to genealogical websites is Cyndi's List <www.cyndislist.com>.

One of the best places to start an online search is at the Family History Library's website <www.familysearch.org>. The Family History Library is the largest genealogical library in the world and is maintained by members of the Church of Jesus Christ of Latter-day Saints (LDS). Initially, search for your earliest-known ancestor. Be sure to explore the learning experiences offered on the site. Later, we'll mention FamilySearch.org as a place to view and learn about original sources. Now, however, at the beginning of your search, FamilySearch.org will be useful in locating family histories, family trees, and ancestors who've found their way into the databases maintained by the LDS church.

Ancestry.com <ancestry.com> has a tremendous collection of resources to help connect you with other people working on the same family lines as you. Access to some of its holdings is free; most content, however, is part of a subscription-based (for a fee) service. Libraries often subscribe to Ancestry.com, so if you're near a library, use Ancestry.com's resources there.

HeritageQuestOnline <heritagequestonline.com> is another popular website that contains more than 28,000 family histories. Libraries often subscribe to this site and access is available at those libraries, but some of those libraries also offer at-home use of HeritageQuestOnline through what's called a "library portal." That is, you must log on to a participating library's site and click on the HeritageQuestOnline link there. Usually you have to enter your library card number to proceed. In addition to the marvelous collection of family histories, HeritageQuestOnline also offers access to the Allen County (Indiana) Public Library's PERSI (PERiodical Source Index). We'll talk more about that later in the section on published articles.

Simply using an Internet search engine can reveal some interesting results. It's helpful to have an ancestor with an uncommon name. Look at the options under "advanced" to make more effective searches. Google has a tremendous collection of mostly out-of-copyright books posted on its site, and they include family and local histories. Just go to <google.com> and then click on Books.

While there's a wonderfully humongous amount of information available on the Internet, everything isn't there yet. But more is added every minute. That's part of why you note the dates of your searches in your research calendar. Internet resources aren't static like printed books. Unless there's a revised or second (or subsequent) edition published, books are pretty much set in stone. Those

Figure 6-1, Title Page and Biographical Entry from a Published Family History:
This entry from a published family history is a gold mine of information for the genealogist.
But remember: Just because it appears in print doesn't mean it's true. Always verify your
information with original source documents.

RECORD

OF THE

RUST FAMILY

EMBRACING THE

DESCENDANTS OF HENRY RUST, WHO CAME FROM ENGLAND AND SETTLED IN HINGHAM, MASS., 1634–1635.

Public Library

By ALBERT D. RUST

OCT 23 1970

Dallas, Texas

"HE THAT WISHES TO BE COUNTED AMONG THE BENEFACTORS OF POSTERITY
MUST ADD BY HIS OWN TOIL TO THE ACQUISITIONS OF HIS ANCESTRY."—RAMBLER.

THOROUGHLY INDEXED.

PUBLISHED BY THE AUTHOR:
WACO, TEXAS.
1891.

149 Thomas Adams[7] (*Jacob Parsons,*[6] *Henry,*[5] *John,*[4] *John,*[3] *Nathaniel,*[2] *Henry*[1]) was born in Salem, 15 Jan., 1798; married first, in Richmond, Va., by Rev. Daniel Roper, 13 May, 1823, Abbie L. Williams, born 26 Feb., 1799; died 8 Oct., 1837; married second, in Richmond, Va., 29 Mar., 1839, by Rev. James B. Taylor, Harriet Willis, daughter of Reuben and Mary Freeman, born 27 Sept., 1817; died 5 Mar., 1844; married third, in Boston, by Rev. R. C. Waterson, 12 May, 1845, Phebe Cutler, daughter of Ephraim and Lydia (Leonard) Chamberlin, of Centre Harbor, N. H., born in Centre Harbor, 11 Sept., 1824. He died at Richmond, Va., 16 Jan., 1882. He was a hardware merchant.

Their children were:

i   Mary Frances,[8] b. 15 June, 1827; d. 27 May, 1829.
ii   Cornelia Lathrop, b. 25 Jan., 1831; m. in Richmond, Va., by Rev. Moses Hodge, 3 Oct., 1850, Woodbury B. Bigelow, b. 5 Oct., 1829. Mr. Bigelow was bookkeeper and Notary Public in and for the State Bank, of Richmond, for eighteen years since the war. He was with the old Farmers' Bank, of Va., thirteen years before the war. He d. 3 Oct., 1888, on the 38th anniversary of his wedding. He was a member of the order A. F. and A. M.; wid. res. 221 S. 3d st., Richmond. They had: i ARCHIBALD BLAIR,[9] (Bigelow) b. 25 July, 1851; m. by Rev. Dr. William Jandrain, 15 Nov., 1887, Miss Blanche Bargamire, of Richmond. He is a bookkeeper. ii MARY WILLIAMS, b. 14 Sept., 1856; m. by Rev. Dr. Moses Hodge, 26 Apr., 1876, Chester A. Delaney. They had: 1 *Josephine.*[10] (Delaney) 2 *Mamie.* 3 *Nellie.* iii WILLIAM M., (Bigelow) b. 15 Aug., 1860. He is a rapid and correct calculator; is entry clerk for a large wholesale house in Richmond; res. 221 South third street.
iii Thomas, b. 15 Oct., 1833; d. 13 Sept., 1834.
iv   Sarah Ann, b. 3 Sept., 1836; d. 21 Jan., 1837.
     (The above are children of first wife.)
v   Henry Freeman, b. 29 Jan., 1840; d. 10 Jan., 1873.
vi   Charles Francis, b. 24 June, 1841; d. 31 July, 1843.
285 vii Edward Freeman, b. 31 Jan., 1843; m. Julia Cabell.
     (The above are children of second wife.)
286 viii Charles Manning b. 12 Feb., 1846; m. Mary L. Wood.
ix   Annie Cooledge, b. 12 Nov., 1847.

Figure 6-2, Country "Mugbooks": Another resource for the genealogist is the published county history, or "mugbook." These books, commonly printed in the 1880s and 1890s, contained not only the history of a county, but biographies of some of its residents. Newton L. Hamm, the subject of this entry, became a "noted resident of Izard County, Arkansas" by paying for the honor, but the real payoff is to his descendants. Newton Hamm's birthdate and birthplace indicate to the genealogist where to seek census records for clues to Newton's ancestors. He owned land, so the researcher knows to check Izard County deed books. The mini-biography even spells out the maiden name of Newton's wife and gives her religious affiliation; the genealogist can now trace her family with church records. Further avenues for pursuit? Newton's church, his Masonic lodge, and his children.

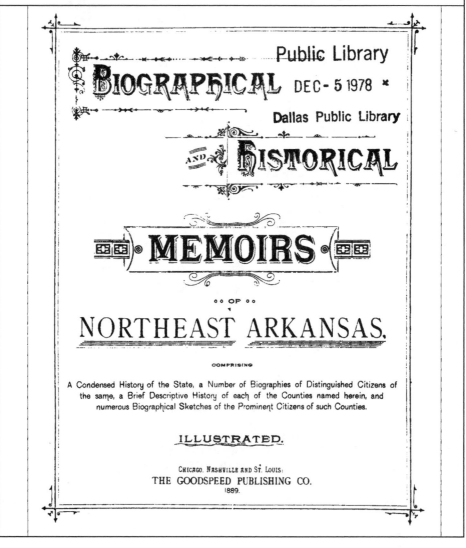

Public Library
DEC - 5 1978

Dallas Public Library

BIOGRAPHICAL

AND HISTORICAL

MEMOIRS

○○ OF ○○

NORTHEAST ARKANSAS,

COMPRISING

A Condensed History of the State, a Number of Biographies of Distinguished Citizens of the same, a Brief Descriptive History of each of the Counties named herein, and numerous Biographical Sketches of the Prominent Citizens of such Counties.

ILLUSTRATED.

CHICAGO, NASHVILLE AND ST. LOUIS:
THE GOODSPEED PUBLISHING CO.
1889.

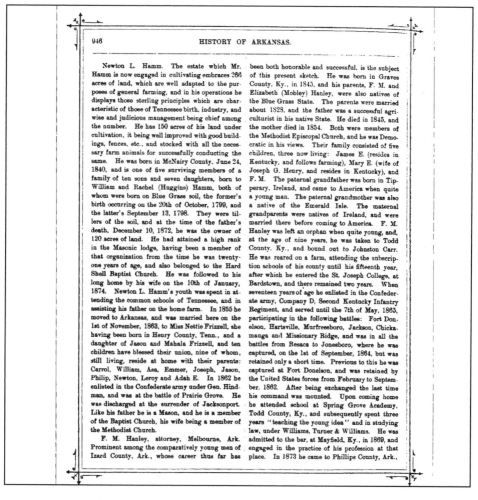

words on the printed page don't change. But words in pixels do. So take the word "research" literally and re-search some of the same online sources on a regular basis.

Eventually, you'll have to climb out of your chair in front of your computer and visit libraries and archives. Yes, gasoline is expensive and time is short; exhaust those readily available Internet sources first. Look at library websites to learn their rules and hours of operation. Archival facilities often post catalogs of their holdings online so you can plan your research excursions. Phone numbers are also posted. You can call and ask about parking and lunch possibilities. You can learn about special holidays, such as Jefferson Davis's Mother's Birthday. Or remodeling schedules.

Libraries are not only a source of published genealogies and genealogical periodicals, they also house volumes of cemetery inventories, books about local history, and many other reference sources essential to genealogists. Archives, on the other hand, are usually repositories for retired official records of public or private agencies. Sometimes, archives also have collections of the same types of books found in libraries. And some libraries maintain collections of manuscript materials, and thus function much like archives.

To find lists of libraries with genealogical collections, do an Internet search for "genealogy libraries." Or visit Cyndi's List: <www.cyndislist.com/libes.htm>. The largest genealogical library in the world is the aforementioned Family History Library in Salt Lake City, Utah. A large portion of that library's as-yet-undigitized collection is available through branch libraries called FamilySearch Centers (also referred to as Family History Centers) located in LDS churches throughout the world. Those local centers offer inexpensive rental of microfilm as a means to view all kinds of books and original records helpful to genealogists. The LDS church does this so genealogists like you will have access to these records without making long, expensive trips to the places where the records are kept. The church couldn't copy everything, however, and you may eventually find yourself making a trip to that ancestral homeland to search for records—but you'll have a head start in the records microfilmed by the Mormons. To learn the location of nearby FamilySearch Centers, visit <www. familysearch.org> and click on the appropriate links.

One part of the Family History Library catalog is devoted to family histories published over the years by genealogists who've compiled the results of their research. The Family History Library has made an effort to collect as many published genealogies as possible. Its holdings of family histories range from small booklets to giant volumes, from amateurs' works to that of renowned professionals. The Family History Library's complete catalog is available through FamilySearch.org.

The Library of Congress in Washington, DC, has thousands of published genealogies in its massive collection. You can search its catalog at <www.loc.gov/rr/genealogy> to learn about books on your family lines.

If you only know the names of your ancestors as far back as your grandparents, you may not readily find a published family history unless one of your cousins has written one. But as you learn more about your family, and discover more and more distant ancestors, the likelihood of finding a published genealogy greatly increases. This phase of searching for published family histories should be repeated every time you discover a new family line or a new set of grandparents.

Remember, just because it's in print doesn't make it true. When you do find a published family history, don't take its contents on faith. And don't let a fancy cover and many reproduced original documents fool you. The author of that volume, no matter how famous and accomplished, may have misinterpreted the information. And if the book was written many years ago, new indexes to source documents may turn up evidence that wasn't accessible when the book was written.

SEARCHING FOR PUBLISHED ARTICLES ABOUT YOUR FAMILY

A tremendous amount of genealogical information has been published in historical and genealogical periodicals. Local historical societies, genealogy clubs, family associations, and ethnic-specific organizations have published thousands of journals, newsletters, magazines, and quarterlies. Some of these periodicals are indexed in each issue, some annually, and a few have cumulative indexes that cover several years. But it's very tedious to figure out which journal might contain an article about your family, then locate back issues in a library so you can make a trip to the library and go through the indexes. There's a better way.

The Allen County (Indiana) Public Library's holdings include a tremendous collection of genealogy periodicals housed at that library, but they aren't online at the library's site. Its comprehensive index, PERSI, and a mail-order form are available through HeritageQuestOnline, a resource described earlier in this chapter. To reiterate, access is through a library "portal." You must visit a participating library's website and click on the HeritageQuestOnline link there. Usually you must enter your library card number.

PERSI has four search options:
- **PEOPLE** for finding personal names,
- **PLACES** for looking up U.S., Canadian, and foreign location names,
- **HOW-TO'S** for identifying articles on research methodology, and
- **PERIODICALS** for searching on a journal title.

PERSI is a subject index, not an every-name index. So an article about the Smith family that contains mention of your ancestor Abner Jones would only list the name Smith in PERSI. But if the title of the article was "Smith Family of Randolph County, North Carolina, 1776–1835," and you knew your Jones family lived in that area during that time period, you'd probably want to read that article. As a subject index, PERSI doesn't contain the text of the articles. But once you know the periodical name and article title, you can obtain photocopies of the entire article by requesting a copy from the holdings of the Allen County Public Library, the Family History Library, or another library whose collection includes the periodical you need. Before you request (and pay for) a copy of an article, search online to see if back issues of that periodical have been digitized and made available online.

Not all family history articles have been published in genealogy periodicals. Some are found in publications outside PERSI's scope. You should use traditional periodical finding aids online and in the reference section of your library to search for family history material in publications not included in PERSI.

SEARCHING FOR FELLOW RESEARCHERS

When you begin your survey of the literature on the subject of your family's history, cross your fingers and hope some remote cousin published some helpful information. It's easier to find than unpublished material. To find the unpublished information, you'll have to search for living cousins who are researching or have worked on discovering your common lineage. These cousins are probably folks you've never met, and you'll discover them as you become a part of the genealogical community.

Genealogists have a lot in common, and when you make contact with a local genealogical or historical society, you'll probably make some really enjoyable friends. These new friends can help you learn about resources and share your enthusiasm about your research.

There's good news and bad news about finding cousins online. The good news is, with the right search terms, you probably can locate any message ever posted online about your family. The bad news is, there may be only an e-mail address as a contact. A defunct e-mail address. But it may not be a total dead end. Persist. Keep reading search results and you may find one from a researcher with a current e-mail address. Search results may take you to message board posts, family websites, blogs, Facebook pages, archived periodicals, and more.

In the old days, we didn't have the Internet and message boards, websites, and convenient ways to look for others working on our family lines. We posted "queries"—short for inquiries—like short ads about who we were working on. Those went into genealogical and historical periodicals as well as newspapers that carried genealogy columns. When the Internet came along, those old materials found their way online, complete with the old queries. Now, they're ten to fifty years old. When you turn up one of those of interest, it's tempting to just dismiss it as too old to follow. Before you do, read the item in this chapter, "Old Queries Never Die."

Your search for fellow researchers doesn't have to be limited to the Internet. Be creative! One researcher left a note in a marriage record volume in a courthouse, stuck in the pages where her ancestor's marriage was recorded. The note said, "If you're related to Bart Abernathy, contact me at (and she included her phone number and e-mail address)." She did this in several courthouses, always being careful to use acid-free paper and penciled notes that wouldn't damage the records. So far, she's had two calls from people who read her notes. One was from a previously unknown cousin, the other from a fellow genealogist who just wanted to tell her how creative she thought the idea was.

When you find someone working on your family lines, remember sharing information is supposed to be a two-way street, a mutual thing. While you may be new and may not have a lot of details about a distant ancestor, you may have current information that would add to a more experienced genealogist's family tree.

What you'll share with cousins is information, and the easiest way to transmit that is with well-documented family group sheets, either on paper or as computer files. Your pedigree chart will also be helpful to show someone your lineage. If you want to be respected as a thorough, competent researcher, include mention of all your sources on your family group sheets. Show where each data item came from. If your correspondents want copies of any of your original materials, they'll ask.

When you receive material from other researchers, ask where they got their information if they don't tell you initially. If they can't supply citations, use their data with great caution. If you incorporate their family information with your own, you'll have to cite the person who gave you the data as the source. Now think about it; the living cousin who says great-grandfather was born in 1875 wasn't an eyewitness, was she? So if she wasn't present, how does she know? Perhaps she copied the date from a gravestone, read it on a death certificate, computed it from his age listed in a federal census record, or found it in the family Bible. Ask how she knows.

Even if you're supplied with undocumented information, you can still use it as research clues. Your source (until you confirm it in other records) is the person who told you or supplied you

Old Queries Never Die

Leslie is an unusual woman, and she uses some unusual genealogical methods in her research. Much to the astonishment of her friends, they usually pay off. Here's Leslie's story about answering a very old query:

"After chasing my great-great grandpa for a roller-coaster six months, I ran into a brick wall, no matter which direction I turned. Was there nothing more I could do? Was I doomed to have ancestry that stopped in 1854?

"Hardly—because old queries never die. Checking back issues of periodicals on the state in which my family had lived, I stumbled across a query on my very own ancestor, a query printed twenty-six years before. In the great scheme of things, twenty-six years is only an instant, I reasoned. I cautiously checked a telephone directory for the town where the long-ago submitter lived (and it was a fairly small town). No surprise there—there was no listing for the name at that address. There was, however, one current listing for that surname in the town, though the first name was different. So I took the plunge and responded to that twenty-six-year-old query to a different person at the wrong address.

"To my astonishment, it worked. Two weeks after I wrote, I received a response from the daughter of the query's author. My letter had gone to her sister-in-law, who had sent it on to her. Her father, she said, was a fearsome genealogist who had pursued our ancestor until the very end of his days. He'd left a wealth of papers to his non-genealogist daughter. She was at a loss as to what to do with them, how to organize the material, or whether to pitch the whole mess.

"Thrilled that someone was interested, she promptly invited me to visit, which I did. I spent a glorious day wallowing in the research files of a cousin whom I'll never meet. Several hours at a copy shop later, I had a ream of information and a brand-new Revolutionary War ancestor—and one who received a pension, at that. I came away with a copy of an original will that had come down through my newly found, deceased cousin's branch of the family. I had information on wives and children in other, related lines, and I had an old list of his correspondents, one of whom I still write to today.

"I've been back to visit several more times. Inexplicably, my new cousin (the daughter) still doesn't do genealogical research, but I've helped her organize the files and arrange to donate them to the genealogy library nearest the family home. I've tried, in part, to repay her father for the help he unknowingly gave me.

"Since then, I've become even more creative about pursuing cold trails. I shamelessly write letters to the editors of small-town newspapers where people in whom I'm interested were reported on the 1920 census. I telephone total strangers who have familiar names in areas where my ancestors lived. I appeal to employees in cemetery and funeral home offices where distant relatives were buried in the hope they'll help me contact the living family members who made the final arrangements. I order death certificates and copies of obituaries of people from whom I'm not descended just to get the names of the living survivors. And all of these radical behaviors have paid off."

For a genealogist, no trail is too faint to follow.

with the facts. One researcher's information shows a great-great-grandfather's death information as "killed in a cornfield in September 1863." Her citation says "Info from a phone call with Cousin Bob Jones, May 25, 1983, who says he heard it from a researcher in Egypt, Arkansas, whose name he can't remember." Boy, is that stretching it!

In addition to exchanging information, you can exchange photos with newly found cousins. They may have photos of your ancestors that have been lost to your branch of the family. And they'll probably want photos of you and your family. It's interesting to look for common physical characteristics.

Remember to label the photos you share. You can write on the backs of traditional resin-coated photo paper with a very soft lead pencil. Record the names of the people or subject of the photo, the date the photo was taken, and your name as the supplier of the photo. Add information to photo computer files by adding comments in their properties boxes. Go to Windows' Help and Support center, then enter "change properties for a file" to learn how.

LOOK FOR ORIGINAL RECORDS

After you assemble and analyze all the sources you can find in your family's possession, seek published books and articles about your family. Then pursue genealogists who are working on your family lines. Once found, exchange information with them. But eventually, you'll reach a stopping point—no more help from fellow researchers, nothing else written about your folks. It's time to direct your search to original records.

You've already encountered original records—remember the birth, marriage, and death certificates you found or requested copies of? The cemeteries you visited where your family members are buried contain original records of a sort. Original records tell us about the events themselves, and it's up to us to examine, evaluate, and analyze those records, then use them to assemble our lineages. We must develop an ear for listening to the documents that may tell us about our ancestors.

Before you go further afield in search of original records, it's a good idea to search online and in library sources for published transcriptions, abstracts, and indexes to original records—sometimes called secondary sources.

> Original records tell us about the events themselves, and it's up to us to examine, evaluate, and analyze those records, then use them to assemble our lineages.

Begin your search for published secondary sources by looking at your family information. Where did they live? The records you need are specific to particular geographic locations. In order to begin research in federal census records, you have to know at least the state in which the family lived during a year the census was taken. To find marriage records, you must guess the county where the marriage took place.

If you create a chronology for your immediate family, you'll probably see many places involved. Perhaps you were

born in one place, grew up in another, went away to college, met your future spouse (who was from somewhere else), returned home to marry, but then you both moved to a faraway place to accept promising jobs. You had children along the way. Your career choices had a lot to do with where you lived. Eventually, you and your spouse built up enough seniority on your jobs to get transferred to a place you wanted to live. Your kids left for college. Retirement planning began, and you bought property in a warm climate. You moved again when retirement came.

Think about how many different places have records about you and your nuclear family. Birth certificates, school transcripts, college diplomas, marriage licenses, rental agreements, deed records, children's birth certificates, employment records, telephone directories, more deed records, tax records, auto and drivers' licenses, Elvis fan club membership cards, insurance policies, vacation mementos, and dozens of other records about you exist in your home and in public places. If you changed spouses, sued someone, ran afoul of the law, or did something newsworthy, you generated even more records.

Even though we're a much more mobile society today, it's the same story for your ancestral families. Some of the records they left are different, but you use them just the same to piece together pictures of their lives.

Don't forget about those groups of people who are also involved with your family; those allied and associated families who were also creating records. Just as your life has touched the lives of others in a wide variety of ways, so did your ancestors' lives.

All of these events in your life and the lives of your ancestors happened in specific geographic places. You must identify these places in order to search for records. You need maps, gazetteers, and atlases to help with your search for place names.

MAPS FOR GENEALOGISTS

Locating place names, especially old ones, can be a real challenge for genealogists. One of the most useful databases of U.S. place names was created by the United States Geological Survey (USGS). It's called the Geographic Names Information System (GNIS).

Employees and contractors created this database by entering all the place names from USGS's most detailed kind of maps, the 7.5 minute topographic maps. They didn't just enter town names, they keyed in all natural features—hills, mountains, streams, rivers, creeks, valleys, knobs, lakes, and others—that had a name. They entered every school, cemetery, crossroads, village, town, city, populated place, and any other manmade feature found on the maps. Then, in phase two of the project, they began to enter place names from old sources, creating a very helpful source for genealogists. If a location went by a different name one hundred years ago, you may find the historical name in the GNIS.

Each entry in the GNIS database lists the place name, its "feature class" (populated place, cemetery, school, lake, stream, etc.), county, geographic coordinate (longitude and latitude description), source coordinate, elevation, and name of the 7.5 minute topographic map on which the place appears. The USGS GNIS database is available for searches on the Internet: <geonames.usgs.gov>.

Other lists of place names, called "gazetteers," are available for a wide range of regions and time periods. *Omni Gazetteer of the United States of America*, an eleven-volume set published by Omnigraphics, is a comprehensive reference tool found in many libraries. For current place names, of course, Google Maps <maps.google.com> is at your fingertips. If you download Google Earth, you can view historical maps for some areas with the "layers" function. Bing Maps <bing.com/maps> is an alternative to Google Maps. A Global Positioning System (GPS) device, either standalone or in a smart phone, is an excellent tool for genealogists.

Maps of all descriptions are good research aids for genealogists. County maps are useful and widely available. Most state highway departments sell county maps for their states, sometimes in two scales. The small scale county maps are ideal to take along on research trips; the large ones allow enough space to write in ancestral land holdings. Most maps from state agencies are inexpensive. The Federal Highway Administration <www.fhwa.dot.gov/webstate.htm> maintains a list of links to state highway departments.

Most of the state mapping agencies or tourism offices offer free highway maps of their states.

Some state mapping agencies have reprinted old maps of their states. Indiana offers an especially nice variety of old map reprints. Alabama's "Old Roads and Traces" map is helpful. Some state mapping agencies sell copies of older versions of their county maps. When you check state websites, always look for reprints of older maps.

Before you order county maps, remember that county boundaries have changed through the years. In 1820, Madison County, Illinois, covered much of the western part of the state. Today, it occupies just a very small area at the southern end of its 1820 boundaries. The best reference source on this subject is William Thorndale and William Dollarhide's *Map Guide to the U.S. Federal Censuses, 1790–1920*. FamilyHistory101.com offers online access to maps illustrating changing county boundaries in the United States <www.familyhistory101.com/maps.html>.

USGS produces a variety of maps. The most detailed are 7.5 minute topographic maps—the ones it used to prepare the GNIS database. These maps show a wonderful level of detail, including relief lines that illustrate elevation. They're inexpensive and available for every area of the United States. Each map covers a small land area, so it usually takes several 7.5 topographic maps to cover a county. Many genealogists, however, can pinpoint the area where their ancestors lived (from deeds and other land records) and may need only one or two to cover the area they're interested in. USGS maps are available from many sources. State mapping agencies often stock them for their states. Hiking shops usually carry them for their areas. Commercial map shops stock them. Go online to <topomaps.usgs.gov/ordering_maps.html> to learn about ordering USGS maps.

If you're interested in old maps, you have some alternatives. You can buy originals from dealers who specialize in old, rare maps. You can buy reprints of old maps from genealogical vendors who list their products on websites. And you can visit libraries and archives who have old maps among their holdings. Most facilities have finding aids describing their maps posted on their websites.

The National Archives has a tremendous map collection. It doesn't produce maps, it just holds, catalogs, and preserves maps created by a wide variety of federal sources, including USGS. There are

Family History Detective

a number of preliminary inventories, special lists, catalogs, and unpublished finding aids that describe some of the map holdings of the National Archives' Cartographic and Architectural Branch. The maps held by the National Archives include those generated by exploration, public land surveys, Indian affairs, navigation, agriculture, topography and natural resources, census mapping, military campaigns, and more. A starting point for the National Archives' most popular maps is <www.archives.gov/research/arc/topics/maps/geographic.html>. Special List 29: List of Selected Maps of States and Territories, an overview of the National Archives' map collection is online at <www.archives.gov/publications/finding-aids/maps>.

The Library of Congress in Washington, DC, also has a tremendous collection of maps. Much of their catalog is online and available through the Internet.

The Library of Congress in Washington, DC, also has a tremendous collection of maps. Much of its catalog is online. Start at <international.loc.gov/ammem/gmdhtml/gmdhome.html> for information about the digitized portion of its collection.

Maps, whether on paper, from an online source, or in a GPS device, are helpful for genealogists who want to find a geographic location. But they're also valuable from another standpoint. Maps help us visualize the territory where our ancestors lived. With maps, we can see surrounding political jurisdictions. When we can't locate a marriage record for an ancestor, we can look at a map and make an educated guess about where that ancestral couple might have gone to obtain a license. Maps help us visualize physical features as well. If a range of mountains separated your ancestors from the area to which they were migrating, we can look at a map and see the route they may have taken around the barrier. When travel was primarily on waterways, maps show us these routes as well.

COUNTY BOUNDARY CHANGES

Identify the places where your ancestors lived. Use maps and gazetteers to find those locations mentioned in your records. Investigate to learn what the political jurisdiction was during the time period your ancestors lived in that place. *Family Tree Sourcebook* by the editors of *Family Tree Magazine* lists all the counties in all the states and gives their creation dates and a description of the territory from which they were created. (The equivalent of counties are called parishes in Louisiana.) The book lists the county seats and mailing addresses of the courthouses. It gives very brief descriptions of the starting dates of major record groups. Capsule histories of the states and brief bibliographies of reference material give you a starting place for research.

In an ideal situation, you should visit the state archives and a major genealogical library in the state where your ancestors lived. Then you should explore the courthouse where your folks went to transact day-to-day business, and you should stop by the local library to examine any records specific to that area. In reality, unless you're very fortunate, you can't do this for all the states where your ancestors lived. Earning a living and family responsibilities have a way of intervening in your genealogical research. What are you going to do?

FINDING SECONDARY SOURCES

After you exhaust online sources, your research efforts may start with the materials available at your local library or the nearest library with a genealogical collection. Then you have to expand your search for secondary sources about the places where your ancestors lived. Visit LDS FamilySearch Centers and seek out libraries within driving distance that have genealogical collections.

Many county histories have been written through the years. During the late 1800s, some companies compiled county histories and included biographical sketches of prominent local citizens. These were often published in regional volumes. They've been reprinted in recent times as genealogical interest in them grew. Many are now available online.

Genealogical societies and individuals have transcribed or compiled indexes to deeds, wills, marriages, tax lists, newspapers, church records, cemeteries, and other records. You can locate these books with traditional search methods in library catalogs. Many libraries have posted their catalogs of holdings on the Internet. You can use the keyword search function on most library websites to find books about specific places. The problem you'll encounter when searching for these kinds of sources is that they were usually published in very small press runs and had a limited distribution. The Family History Library in Salt Lake City has made a special effort to search out and acquire these works. Its catalog files them in the "locality" listings.

Secondary, or compiled, sources shouldn't be used instead of primary sources. Most compilers advise readers to use their books as finding aids to original records. Secondary sources should never be used to determine that a record doesn't exist. When a listing doesn't appear in an index, it means nothing more than you didn't find it in the index. It doesn't even mean the entry wasn't in the index. It may be there, but under a spelling variation you missed. When you don't find an entry for a particular person in a census index, it doesn't mean that person isn't listed in the census records themselves.

> Many libraries have posted their catalogs of holdings on the Internet. You can use the keyword search function on most library websites to find books about specific places.

Secondary sources are often indexes or lists of names. Be careful that you don't abandon your search for people and begin a search for names. Maintain your search for groups of people, not just one individual.

ETIQUETTE

When you venture into libraries and archives in search of family information, follow their regulations. In many facilities, you'll be given a list of the rules when you register. Often you'll be required to show identification to obtain a researcher's card.

Your personal belongings may be examined before and after you use the library. The rules are in place for a purpose, and your cooperation will expedite your research.

Staff members are often overworked and underpaid. Do ask them for information, but be brief with your questions. Don't tell family stories. If a librarian needs more information about your family in order to point you toward the right resources, she'll ask. When you ask for information, listen to the answer. Listen carefully, then ask for clarification if you need it. If you're expected to reshelve the books you use, do so. If you're only allowed five photocopies before returning to the end of the copier line, only do five. If you're directed to use only pencils for writing, use a pencil.

Research time is often limited, especially for people who've driven a long way to use the library. Don't take up your fellow researchers' time with your family stories or extended complaints about library rules or personnel.

Wear appropriate clothing. Though it sounds unfair, your attire can have an impact on your success in a library. Staff members are people, and people often make judgments about others based upon how they're dressed. The person in the business suit may be offered more assistance than the one in shorts and T-shirt.

Remember your manners—say please and thank you, take turns, obey the rules—and you'll have a more pleasant research experience.

KEY CLUES

- Broaden your search to unknown distant cousins, published genealogies, online databases, and libraries and archives only after you've exhausted your home sources and knowledgeable relatives.
- Helpful genealogy websites include <www.cyndislist.com>, <www.familysearch.org>, <ancestry.com>, and <heritagequestonline.com> (available only through public libraries).
- Search for published genealogies about your family on Google books <books.google.com> or the Library of Congress <www.loc.gov/rr/genealogy>.
- Use the United States Geological Survey (USGS) Geographic Names Information System (GNIS) <geonames.usgs.gov> to search for information about where your ancestors lived.
- Find maps that illustrate the changes that have occurred in county boundaries in the United States at <www.familyhistory101.com/maps.html>.
- Be courteous and obey the rules when visiting libraries. Respect the librarian's time.

YOU CAN'T HAVE ONE WITHOUT THE OTHER
History and Genealogy

Genealogy and history are intertwined. In order to understand your ancestors, you have to learn more about the times and events that surrounded their lives. Without historical context, genealogy can get pretty dry. A collection of names and dates doesn't explain who your ancestors were.

Reading history can bring your ancestors to life. They were part of the social, economic, religious, and political events of their time. There's an added benefit—reading history can help you solve genealogical problems. When you can't find a previous residence for an ancestor, read about the factors that caused migration to the area where you know your ancestor lived. Learn where other people came from and why they came. Chances are, your problem of the previous residence will be solved.

When you begin your genealogy search, you're looking for tiny bits of data, small clues. You only want a single marriage record out of dozens performed that year in a particular place. You're after the deed records for your great-grandfather, so you sift through hundreds of other land records. Cautioned to look for details, you go about this project with a magnifying glass. Keep on, and you'll miss the big picture.

Step back from your research and use a wide-angle lens. Look at the big picture. See your ancestors as part of something larger. Read about all aspects of history.

A READING PLAN

So many books, so little time. How are you going to pick and choose what you want to read to supplement your genealogy? Some topics, such as marriage, death, social customs, migration patterns, and local history are something all genealogists have in common. Beyond the broad topics, special interest takes over, and you have to select books about topics that tell you more about your ancestors.

Consider your ancestors' lives. When did they live? Where? If your earliest American ancestor was Irish and came over during the potato famines of the 1840s, you probably aren't interested in colonial American history. Assess the information you have about your family members. Don't just concentrate on the distant past. If your father served in the military during World War II and your mother worked in a defense plant, do some reading about that event. It probably had a major impact on their lives. If they're alive, ask about personal recollections, then supplement those reminiscences with reading.

Your grandparents may have left the Midwest during the Great Depression and migrated to California. Read about those times and learn what caused them to load up all their belongings and move half a continent away. Historians have written extensively about our past. All you have to do is find the books and articles.

It isn't always easy. Finding materials of interest requires research. If your library's catalog is online, use the keyword search and enter topics of interest. Check the reference department of your library for *Harvard Guide to American History*, compiled by Frank Freidel. It's a bit dated, but a good place to start. This set contains bibliographies arranged by topic. Or just google the topic you're interested in, such as "Irish potato famine."

Talk with the reference librarian and ask about finding aids for humanities subjects. She'll explain the resources available in your library.

Once you locate a book or article on a subject you're interested in, pay attention to the footnotes and bibliography. An author who does a thorough job tells you about sources for the material used in writing the book. Start a list of books you want to find, based on bibliographies in the volumes you've found. You have been advised to keep a research calendar of the genealogical sources you're searched—you can do the same for history books and articles. And you can list the books and journal articles on that list that you want to read, as well.

In the genealogical field, we're lucky to have PERSI (described in Chapter 6). The only index in the field of history that approaches the comprehensiveness of PERSI is *America: History and Life*. This database is offered through some library websites.

When you find a citation to an article in an historical journal, check to see if your library owns copies of the back issues for that title. If not, search to see if those back issues have been posted online. Failing that, talk to the interlibrary loan specialist about ordering a photocopy of the article. Sometimes you're required to pay for photocopies, but often there's no charge for this service.

You also can use interlibrary loan to obtain the history books of interest to you. Ask about your library's policy—sometimes there's a charge for the service. It's often difficult to find an interlibrary loan source for genealogy books, but history books were published in larger press runs and are more readily available.

A good strategy for reading history to supplement your genealogy is to start with a broad overview, then narrow your reading. Begin with a history of the United States. You can scan a high school or college textbook for a refresher course on political history.

To learn more about social history, try Daniel J. Boorstin's trilogy about American social history, *The Americans*. The first of the three volumes, *The Americans: The Colonial Experience*, describes life in early America. Boorstin writes about the people—Quakers, Puritans, Virginians—and the kinds of communities they established. He writes about the legal profession, medicine, science, language, and books.

In the second volume, *The Americans: The National Experience*, he describes New Englanders who made fortunes from granite and ice, the people who migrated westward in such haste, boosters and builders who created new communities, and the black and white Southerners. In the third volume, *The Americans: The Democratic Experience*, Boorstin writes about range wars, divorce, gambling, crime, standardized clothing, advertising, food preservation, snake oil remedies, grammar, and other social history topics. Best of all, all three volumes contain excellent bibliographical essays that lead you to other sources. These three volumes were so popular that Amazon.com offers used copies for pennies (plus shipping, of course).

NARROW YOUR FOCUS

After the overview, narrow your focus to the time and place of your ancestors' lives. If they were among the millions who pushed the American frontier westward, read two books by Ted Morgan, *Wilderness at Dawn: The Settling of the North American Continent* and *A Shovel of Stars: The Making of the American West 1800 to the Present*. Morgan isn't a professional historian like many writers of history—his works read like adventure tales. His second volume offers great detail about states' territorial periods.

One of the best books on American migrations westward is Ray Allen Billington's *Westward Expansion: A History of the American Frontier*. The book has been through several editions and can be found in libraries and through Amazon.com or AbeBooks.com. It contains a thorough bibliography, annotated with Billington's comments about the sources.

Your interest may be in a specific ethnic group. If your ancestors are Irish, German, Jewish, Italian, Chinese, Japanese, African-American, Puerto Ricans, or Mexicans, start with Thomas Sowell's *Ethnic America: A History*. In a wonderfully readable style, he talks about the push-pull factors that brought these groups to the United States. He calls the peopling of America "one of the great dramas of human history."

Then search for more specific books that only deal with the people you're descended from. Probably your ancestors were a mixture of several ethnic groups. Read about them. Read about the political and social history of the countries from which they came.

If your ancestors were Scots-Irish, for example, you might start with *The Scotch-Irish: A Social History* by James G. Leyburn. It's an older work (1962) and paints a picture of these hardworking, industrious people who always managed to be on the edge of civilization. For an alternate view of the same folks, try Grady McWhiney's *Cracker Culture: Celtic Ways in the Old South*. His Scots-Irish were hardworking people who preferred the frontier to get away from governmental interference.

> Probably your ancestors were a mixture of several ethnic groups. Read about them. Read about the political and social history of the countries from which they came.

Move your reading from the particular ethnic group to the time and place where they settled. Robert W. Ramsey's *Carolina Cradle: Settlement of the Northwest Carolina Frontier, 1747–1762* describes not only the Scots-Irish, but also the other ethnic groups with whom they came into contact in the backwoods. My family picked up some interesting genes when a backwoods Baptist married into the Society of Friends (Quakers).

If you have ancestors in any of four particular migrations of people from the British Isles to America, you'll enjoy David Hackett Fischer's *Albion's Seed: Four British Folkways in America*. He thoroughly describes four waves of English-speaking immigrants who came to America between 1629 and 1775. The first were the Puritans from the east of England to Massachusetts Bay. The second were the Royalist elite and their indentured servants from the south of England to Virginia. The third was that of the Quakers or Society of Friends who came to the Delaware Valley. And the fourth was the flight from the borderlands of northern Britain and northern Ireland who came to the American backcountry. This fourth group is called the Scots-Irish on this side of the Atlantic. These four groups of people brought their own customs, folkways, attitudes, rituals, traditions, and ways of life.

This list of books could go on and on. Discussion of these mentioned is just to give you an idea of the kinds of books available that will help you understand your ancestors. Full citations for the examples I gave are listed in the resource section.

FAMOUS RELATIVES

If you have an ancestor who was famous or associated with a famous person, read more about them. One researcher mentioned a family legend that her ancestor had been a body slave to Robert E. Lee, the Confederate general. She read several biographies of General Lee to learn about his farm, his lifestyle, and his slaves. Her ancestor wasn't mentioned by name in the books, but she knows from her reading what her ancestor's life must have been like.

Drawing a Timeline to Find Soldier Ancestors

Who were your ancestors who might have served in America's wars? Right off, it may be a bit difficult to correlate dates of events with your ancestors' lives. Sometimes your brain needs a little help organizing information. If you create a diagram, it may help you see things a bit differently. Try the following technique and see if it works for you. If it helps clarify your thinking about your potential-soldier ancestors, apply it to other subjects.

Remember in school when you had to make a timeline for some history assignment? Let's try it again. Tape some sheets of paper together, end to end, and draw a heavy line horizontally down the middle of them. Use a ruler and establish a scale. You might make one inch equal five years. Label the right end of the heavy line "the present." Mark the line off in increments and label them to suit your scale. Mark the decades on the heavy line—1990, 1980, 1970, and so on, backward in time for a couple of centuries. Then, above the heavy line, label the major U.S. wars on your timeline, working back to the Revolutionary War.

Underneath the heavy line and parallel to it, draw another line representing your life. Begin the line at the year of your birth and draw it parallel to the heavy line on which you marked the dates. Drop down just a bit and do the same for your father's life span. If he's living, extend the line to the present, starting it at his birth year. Do the same for your grandfathers. And for your four great-grandfathers. Consult the family group sheets and pedigree chart you've compiled. You may not know the exact

War or Conflict	Dates
Vietnam	1954–1975
Korea	1950–1953
World War II	1939–1945
World War I	1914–1918
Spanish-American War	1898–1899
Civil War	1861–1865
Mexican War	1846–1848
War of 1812	1812–1815
Revolutionary War	1776–1783

birth and death dates of all these men, so make an educated guess if you must, for now. Leave off your ancestors who never came to America. You'll have to consider their participation in wars in their native countries.

You've been drawing parallel lines so far, the heavy one representing the continuum of time and others representing the years of your male ancestor's lives. (We're just doing the guys in this exercise because soldiers were primarily male, especially in historic times.) Now use a highlighter or marker and draw a sweep of color vertically through the heavy line where you've marked off the war time periods, on through your ancestors' lines. Your object is to highlight the time periods in their lives when the wars occurred. Now compute their ages at the time of the wars from your heavy line. Some will have been children or older men during wartime. Any of the men who fall within possible military age on your timeline may have served in the military.

There's free software on the Internet to create timelines. Do a search for "Timeline creation free software." Timelines are fairly straightforward creations, however, and you can do it without computer assistance. It's a good way to involve children in genealogy.

Remember when you're looking at ancestors' lives that military age is relative. Henry N. Walls was born in 1901. He was too young to be required to register for the draft before World War I. His older brother got to go, but Henry didn't. He tried to enlist, but the recruitment officer knew the family and told him his mother's signature would be required. Henry's widowed mother had no intention of allowing her youngest to volunteer, so he missed out on the war. When World War II came along in 1941, he was past 40, too old to be drafted. But he enlisted anyway in the U.S. Navy's Seabees, a construction battalion. His father, James Henry Walls, nearly missed the Civil War. Born in 1846, he didn't turn 18 until 1864. The war was still on when he became eligible, so he enlisted and spent the last year of the war in service. Allow a little latitude in your estimate of "military age."

Drawing the timeline allows you to see the information about your family in a different way. You can use this technique for other historical events and include your female ancestors as well.

The famous person in your family may have been a collateral ancestor, someone related to you but not someone you're descended from. Investigate! Remember that family stories have a way of becoming distorted through the years. You may not be descended from Andrew Jackson (he didn't have children of his own), but if that story has been handed down in your family, look to see if you're related to the extensive Donaldson clan, the family of Jackson's wife. Or find out if you descended from another of Jackson's relations. A story has an origin somewhere, so don't discard it out-of-hand when it doesn't seem true upon your initial examination.

Remember, too, that everyone (well, nearly everyone) wants to have a connection to famous or heroic historical figures. Or infamous people. Hundreds of families throughout the Midwest have a family legend that goes something like this: "One night Jesse James came to the house with his band of outlaws. Grandpa let them sleep in his barn and they gave him a gold piece they stole in their last train robbery." Maybe an outlaw did sleep in Grandpa's barn, and *maybe* it was Jesse James. Read about outlaws in post-Civil War Missouri. Read a biography of Jesse James.

WAR AND OTHER MOMENTOUS EVENTS

Some of the momentous events in the nation's history have involved our participation in wars. You may be a Vietnam War veteran. Your father or uncles (or you yourself) may have served in Korea or World War II. Your grandfather may have served in World War I. And his grandfather may have served in the Civil War.

A timeline is a way to pinpoint your ancestors who were of an age to have served in American wars. Once you identify the wars in which your ancestors might have been involved, you can search for military records (and that's the topic of another book). In the meantime, read about those wars. For the recent wars, you may have information about your family member's participation.

Think about your ancestors' lives and what happened during the time they were alive. Which people in your family might have been excited about the news of the discovery of gold in California in 1849? Did the stock market crash of 1929 have an impact on your relatives? What happened to your ancestors during the Great Depression? Did the great flood of the Mississippi River in 1927 affect your family?

Besides specific events, there are some topics of interest to genealogists in general and those deal with the facts of our ancestors' lives. Marriages, divorces, deaths, funerals, and inheritance are topics that have been widely written about by social historians.

MARRIAGE RECORDS

When you looked for a marriage record in a courthouse, did you just look for your family members? Just the ones with the surname you're interested in? More experienced genealogists also pull out the records for collateral relatives, those descendants of long-forgotten aunts and uncles, brothers and sisters of their ancestor.

You can do more. Study that set of records. Look up the minister's credentials. In order to perform marriage ceremonies, ministers and other religious leaders had to bring evidence to the county clerk's office of their position in their religious body. Those credentials had to be transcribed into the county record books by the clerk. They usually identify the church or religious group that had conferred the status of minister. The records of that group may contain helpful genealogical information.

When you study that volume of marriage records, look at what's happening. If ages are recorded in that time and place, what is the average age at which women and men are marrying? Is your ancestor older or younger than average? Look at the age difference between most brides and grooms—is the age difference different for your ancestral couple? Are there many marriages for senior citizens? What's going on in the community represented by those records?

Backing up ever further from the records, do some reading about marriage customs. David Freeman Hawke's *Everyday Life in Early America* briefly describes marriage customs. In Virginia, for example, he says a Southern wedding was a festive affair, followed by card playing, dancing, "an elegant supper," and singing. In New England, however, the Congregationalists had a different view. They saw it as a civil affair, officiated by a magistrate. Do some reading and learn about the customs involved in courtship and marriage for the time and place where your ancestors lived.

People in previous years divorced for many of the same reasons people file divorces today. Divorce rates did vary by region.

DIVORCE

You may encounter a divorce in your family. Don't let anyone tell you how rare it used to be. People in previous years divorced for many of the same reasons people file divorces today. Divorce rates did vary by region; they were lower in the South and higher in the

West. And they were probably lower among some religious groups whose tenets especially forbade divorce. But they did happen. And they left records that often give a great amount of insight into family life.

To learn more about the subject of divorce, read Glenda Riley's *Divorce: An American Tradition*. Some of the information she relates about divorce laws is important when you begin a search of the records. Suppose, for example, a man disappears from the records, leaving a wife and children behind. You can't find a death record, no settlement of his estate, no divorce in the local records—just a missing husband. There's nothing in the records that actually says the woman is a widow, but you want to explain the disappearance. The information in Riley's book brings up an interesting possibility. The missing man may have left for the frontier—moved out west in search of gold, adventure, new possibilities. After fulfilling a short residency requirement in his new home, he could have obtained a divorce on grounds of desertion—hers, not his. Thus the records would be in some faraway place. But without reading about the topic of divorce, you might not consider all the possibilities.

DEATH WAYS

One of the great preoccupations of genealogists is finding death records. You want those ancestors to live again by re-creating their lives, and you want to know when they died. It's often helpful to learn about the customs involved in funerals and burial to help you decide what kinds of records might be available to supply death dates. Reading books and articles about social history can help.

Look for sources about the time and place where your ancestors lived. If they lived in the Southern uplands you might read James K. Crissman's *Death and Dying in Central Appalachia: Changing Attitudes and Practices*. In it, he describes how mountain people felt about commercial funerals. They buried their own dead, with the neighbors helping to prepare the body for burial, until well into the mid-twentieth century. Predictably then, there was high noncompliance with the laws requiring death registration. Reading can give you clues to cemetery locations. In the upland South, Crissman quotes an older settler as saying graveyards were always located on high ground, never in valleys.

Your selection of reading material on this subject will be dictated by where your ancestors lived. When you visit a large library or use an online catalog, search under keywords for terms such as "funeral rites and ceremonies." Then look for material on your region and time period of interest.

A more general book on funeral homes and burial customs is *The History of American Funeral Directing*, by Robert W. Habenstein and William M. Lamers. It's not new, published in 1955, and probably only available through libraries and online used-book sellers, but it's filled with details about funeral customs and corpse preservation. If you wonder what the funeral ceremony was like for an ancestor who died in Victorian times, books like this one can supply minute details.

We're concerned with where our ancestors are buried, so cemeteries are an interesting subject for genealogists. David Charles Sloane's *The Last Great Necessity: Cemeteries in American History*, describes the kinds of cemeteries used in America from frontier graves to well-tended memorial parks. Today, when we walk through a cemetery, we don't think much about trends in markers or why the place was selected as a cemetery site, but learning the history behind those places can furnish information about your family. If the cemetery is a commercial enterprise, someone bought the plot where your family is buried; records should be available.

Historical society journals often contain articles about particular cemeteries. They don't often contain complete inventories of the interments; those are left to genealogical periodicals. To locate a history of the cemetery you're interested in may require a afternoon of reading tables of contents in back issues of the historical society's quarterly if they aren't posted online.

INHERITANCE

You're interested in inheritance because the records involved often supply the links between generations. When people leave wills naming their children, it greatly simplifies your research task. A study by three historians, Carole Shammas, Marylynn Salmon, and Michel Dahlin, can help your understanding of this subject. *Inheritance in America: From Colonial Times to the Present* was first published by Rutgers University Press in 1987.

Laws about inheritance changed over time, and they differed greatly from place to place in the United States. Reading about the laws can help you decide which records to look for and what they mean.

Learning about the legal system in general, not just as it pertains to inheritance, can be of great benefit to you. If you want to start with an overview on the topic, read Lawrence M. Friedman's *A History of American Law.*

Learning about the legal system in general, not just as it pertains to inheritance, can be of great benefit to you.

EXPAND YOUR READING

So many books, so little time. It's difficult to choose a starting place, so start with some volumes that will give you a broad overview, then narrow your focus. Keep pursuing footnotes. Maintain your list of books and articles to pursue. The resource section in this volume contains more suggestions for the kinds of titles you might read and full citations for the books mentioned in this book.

SOURCES FOR BOOKS

Your local library (including its interlibrary loan department) is your best source for the books mentioned. But we're acquisitive people, aren't we? You'll probably want to own some of your favorite books. And you may find some books of continuing value to you, so you'll want the convenience of having them in your home library.

Here are some tips on sources for books. You can buy them new from traditional and online bookstores, of course, but only so long as they're in print and available from the publisher. Amazon.com, AbeBooks.com, and other booksellers offer used books. Libraries often hold used book sales. Join the Friends group for your library so you won't miss any sale announcements. Watch for notices about antiquarian book shows in your area. When the term "used" turns to "antiquarian," the prices go up, but the selection gets more interesting.

Build your personal library of historical titles as a sideline to your genealogy. But whether you choose to borrow or buy books, continue to read about history to increase your understanding of your ancestors' lives and the events that surrounded them.

KEY CLUES

- Research historic topics, both recent and distant, that directly impacted your family.
- If you have an ancestor who was famous or associated with a famous person, read more about them.
- Search for marriage records for collateral relatives to find more allied families.
- Research the credentials of the ministers who performed your ancestors' weddings. You may find new church records to research.

TAKING NAMES
Finding Census Records

Remember when the last federal census was taken? The government made a huge publicity effort to let everyone know how it important it was to participate. The questions they asked weren't the same as in previous census years. Local government officials argued their areas were under reported. Finally, the numbers were in and it all blew over.

This description could have been written after any of the federal censuses since 1790, when the first one counted the inhabitants of the United States. In the name of equal representation, the Constitution mandated census taking every ten years.

Census records are like a snapshot of the entire nation. The information gathered varied from census to census, but essentially, the process gives us a look at where everyone in the United States was as of a particular day. Or it was supposed to, anyway. The records accumulated by the census taking haven't all survived. There were flaws in the system, but taken as a whole, federal census records are one of the most helpful bodies of records genealogists can use.

If you were to survey experienced genealogists on the topic of which single group of records is the most helpful for family history research, census records would top the list. They're a mainstay of genealogical research, and for that reason an entire chapter is devoted to them in this book.

In this chapter, you'll see the information available in each census year's records, and you'll see census records used in a case study on the Cates family. As you read about them, think of your family and apply the same research methodology when you're ready to venture into census records. You'll learn how to focus on your family's records.

First, a little background about the agencies responsible for creating the records may be helpful. The Constitution's directive that a census should be taken didn't offer specifics about who should do the job. From 1790 through 1840, federal marshals did it. They weren't necessarily the best-qualified people for the job, nor were they offered much training. They didn't even get preprinted forms until 1830. Pay was low and the job was tough.

For the 1850 census, a Census Bureau office was established in Washington, DC. The focus of census entries shifted from the family to the individual. Instead of devoting one line to a family, listing only the head of that family, the census in 1850 listed every person on a separate line in the returns. The Census Bureau was a temporary agency, resurrected every ten years to tend to the counting. It wasn't until 1902 that a permanent Bureau of the Census was created as part of the Department of the Interior, then transferred to the Department of Commerce.

THE CENSUS OF 1790

The 1790 federal census lists the names of the heads of households. People within each family were divided into the following categories: free white males of sixteen years and upwards, free white males under sixteen years, free white females, all other free persons, and slaves. The census was started on August 2, 1790, but it took until March 1792, to finish the job.

American Indians weren't included in the census unless they were living as part of Anglo-American communities. If they were living with their tribal groups, they were considered "Indians not taxed," and weren't counted. The "all other free persons" category referred to persons considered "free people of color," that is, people who obviously weren't white, but were not enslaved.

The assistant marshals who did the enumeration were directed to copy their returns and post the copies in two public places in their assigned areas, so people could check them for errors. Then they forwarded them to the president.

Only about two-thirds of the 1790 census records survived. The existing records have been transcribed, indexed, and published by the Bureau of the Census in 1908, as *Heads of Families at the First Census of the United States Taken in the Year 1790*, a twelve-volume set available in many libraries. It's available online at <www.census.gov/prod/www/abs/decennial/1790.html>. This version is an alphabetized typescript of all the existing records. The original records themselves are available as a National Archives microfilm publication. For some states where the records are missing, tax lists have been published as substitutes.

THE CENSUS OF 1800

The official date of the 1800 census was August 4. Beginning with the 1800 census, the federal marshals reported to the secretary of state, instead of directly to the president. In 1800, the marshals counted people in a more detailed breakdown by age than had been done in 1790. They counted free white males and females in age categories of 0 to 10, 10 to 16, 16 to 20, 16 to 26, 26 to 45, and 45 and older. They counted the number of other free persons, the number of slaves, and they listed the town or district and county of residence. Most of the schedules were reported in the order in which they were enumerated, giving genealogists information about the people who lived near their ancestors.

THE CENSUS OF 1810

In 1810, the census was started August 6. The 1810 census was much like that of 1800. In this enumeration, marshals inquired about manufacturing establishments.

THE CENSUS OF 1820

The official starting date for the 1820 census was August 7. For the first time, the marshals got printed instructions about how to conduct the census.

The reporting age categories were the same as the previous census, except for the addition of a category for free white males ages 16 to 18. The new nation, having just come through a second war with Britain, needed to know what its potential military strength was. The men counted in this category were supposed to also be included in the broader category of white males "of 16 and under 26," but there was some confusion about it.

This census also counted the number of persons not naturalized (non-citizens), giving researchers some hints about when a family had immigrated to the United States. The number of people engaged in agriculture, commerce, and manufacture were counted.

In this census, the manufacturers' schedules, separate from the population schedules, listed the owner's name, location of the business, number of employees, type of equipment, amount of capital invested, articles manufactured, annual production figures, and remarks about the business.

THE CENSUS OF 1830

The date of the census for 1830 changed from a traditional August date to June 1. For genealogists, that means there aren't ten full years between the census of 1820 and that of 1830. Thus a person born in June or July of 1820, who fell in the 0 to 10 age category in that census, might still be counted as under 10 years old as of June 1, 1830. The situation applies to some other age categories as well. The window of probability for this affecting one of your ancestors is small, but exists, nevertheless.

The June 1 date became the official census date through the 1900 census. For the census of 1830, the marshals were furnished for the first time with printed, blank forms to record answers.

The age categories for free white males and free white females were further broken down: 0 to 5, 5 to 10, 10 to 15, 15 to 20, 20 to 30, 30 to 40, 40 to 50, 50 to 60, 60 to 70, 70 to 80, 80 to 90, 90 to 100, and over 100 years. Age categories for free colored males and free colored females were: under 10, 10 to 23, 24 to 35, 36 to 54, 55 to 99, and over 100 years. Male slaves and female slaves were broken down in the same age categories as free colored persons. The 1830 census was the first to include a column with the total number of persons in the household.

The question about "foreigners not naturalized" was asked. And questions were asked about the numbers of "deaf, dumb, and blind" persons in each household.

THE CENSUS OF 1840

The census age categories remained the same as those of 1830. In this census, however, for the first time, the names and ages of Revolutionary War pensioners were provided. The questions about occupations were expanded to include mining; agriculture; commerce; manufacturing and trade; navigation of the ocean; navigation of canals, lakes, and rivers; and "learned professions" and engineers. Questions were asked about the number of people in school and the number in the family who were over age 21 and could not read and write. The marshals also asked about the number of "insane" people, and they were supposed to distinguish between those in private care and those in public charge.

THE CENSUS OF 1850

The census reports underwent a tremendous change in 1850. Every person was enumerated on a separate line in the returns, not just one family per line. The model for this census was one done in Boston in 1845, and it's of tremendous benefit to genealogists. The following information is listed for each person: name; age at last birthday; sex; race; profession or occupation; value of real estate; place of birth; whether newlywed; if attended school within the year; if the person could not read and write; if the person was deaf, dumb, blind, insane, or idiotic; and if the person was a convict or pauper.

Slaves were enumerated on separate schedules (Slave Schedules) in 1850 and 1860. The name of the slave owner is listed, but the given names of the slaves aren't. Instead, they're identified by age, color, sex, and whether they were deaf-mute, blind, insane, or idiotic; and whether or not they were a fugitive from the state.

A note should be added here about some of the terms used in old records. We don't call hearing-impaired people with a speech impediment "deaf and dumb" anymore. We don't refer to mentally disabled people as "idiots." (Of course, we're going to reach a point where bald people are "combing-impaired" or "follicle-ly challenged.") But some of the words in old records are offensive to some people. If we change the words or labels, we may change the meaning of the information, so we're forced to leave offensive terms such as "colored" in place. Remind the people you share your information with that the words aren't yours. Be careful not to apply today's definitions to yesterday's words. "Insane" in 1850 may have been applied to someone who drank alcohol to excess or had a severe case of PMS.

Birthplaces listed in the 1850 census were the state, territory, or country; nothing more specific is usually given. Sometimes an examination of the birthplaces of a list of children in a family will show a migration pattern. The family's oldest children may list North Carolina as their birthplace;

their nearest siblings may show Tennessee, and the youngest members of the family may have been born in Missouri, the place of residence of the family. By looking at the ages of the children, you can compute the dates they moved from one state to another.

Relationships between the members of the household aren't stated in the 1850, 1860, or 1870 censuses. A man, woman, and group of children may be a nuclear family, but that is only implied, and needs additional proof. Dwelling and household numbers are listed in the census. Each separate dwelling house received a number and there may have been more than one individual family under that roof.

In 1850, the first mortality schedules were compiled. Census enumerators asked each family if anyone had died there within the twelve months prior to June 1. If so, the deceased person was listed on a separate schedule. Information collected included the deceased's name, age, sex, color, whether widowed, place of birth, month of death, occupation or trade, cause of death, and the number of days ill. Mortality schedules, while taken at the same time as the population schedules, have been separated from them through the years, and the records exist in a variety of places. Several indexes have been published to the existing mortality schedules and can be located when searching the records of a particular locality. Mortality schedules accompany the censuses of 1850, 1860, 1870, and 1880.

THE CENSUS OF 1860

The census of 1860 is much like that of 1850, though there are a few differences. The post office address is at the top of each census page in 1860. In addition to the value of real estate, a separate column in 1860 lists the value of personal property.

THE CENSUS OF 1870

The census of 1870 was a repeat of 1860 with a few minor changes. In the column asking if a couple had been married within the year prior to the taking of the census, the enumerator in 1870 was supposed to write the month of the marriage. If a person was born within the year, the month of birth was supposed to be written in. If the parent of a person listed was of foreign birth, that was supposed to be noted in the appropriate column. The question as to whether someone was a convict or pauper was dropped. Slave schedules, of course, were discontinued. "Color" designations were supposed to be recorded more precisely: white (W), black (B), Chinese (C), Indian (I), mulatto (M). "Indian" meant American Indian, not someone from India.

THE CENSUS OF 1880

In 1880, the census underwent another big change. From a genealogist's standpoint, things got even better. Most all the same questions from 1850, 1860, and 1870 returns were retained, but there were important additions. For the first time, the relationships of people to the head of each household were recorded. Enumeration districts were listed, and in urban areas, street and house numbers were given.

The birthplaces of each person's mother and father (state, territory, or country) are listed. It's secondhand information, but usually leads you in the right direction. Marital status is listed for the first time. Questions about the value of real and personal property were dropped. The question from 1870 about whether the parents were of foreign birth wasn't needed since birthplaces of parents were now listed.

THE CENSUS OF 1890

Unfortunately, all but 1 percent of the population schedules of the 1890 federal census were destroyed in the aftermath of a fire near Washington, DC, in 1921.

About half of a special veterans schedule did survive the fire. The veterans schedules that survive start in the middle of the reports for Kentucky and continue alphabetically through the states (so only the records for states L–W exist).

Each entry lists the Union Civil War veteran's name, widow's name, his rank, company, regiment, dates of service, post office address, disability, and remarks. Sometimes Confederate veterans were listed, too, though often their names have a single line drawn through them on the reports, however they are still legible in most cases.

THE CENSUS OF 1900

The population schedules for 1900 were even more detailed than those of previous years. Month and year of birth are listed for each person. In addition to marital status, the number of years married, total number of children born to a mother, and the number of those children who were living at the time of the census are listed. This can help you identify potential birth and death records you many need to search for.

The year of immigration and number of years in the U.S. are shown for foreign-born people. Questions were asked about whether the family's home was on a farm, and whether the home or farm was owned (and, if so, whether or not it was mortgaged) or rented.

THE CENSUS OF 1910

Since 1830, June 1 had been the official census date. In 1910, however, the date changed to April 15. The 1910 census dropped the question about month and year of birth. It added, for foreign-born people, a question about their native language. This census also shows whether someone was a Civil War veteran or the widow of one.

THE CENSUS OF 1920

The date of the 1920 census was set as January 1. Though it was much like the 1910 census, it dropped the questions about Union or Confederate military veterans, number of children, and duration of marriage.

It added questions about the year of naturalization, and the "mother" tongue of the person and both of his parents. It asked the year of arrival for non-native-born people.

THE CENSUSES OF 1930 AND BEYOND

The government has promised census records will remain confidential for seventy-two years after they're taken. That means the release date for the 1940 census should be in 2012.

The 1930 census is much like 1920. Additional questions were asked about employment. The 1940 census was the first to employ sampling, an advanced statistical technique. Enumerators in 1940 asked even more questions than in 1930 about unemployment, internal migration, and income. It was the first to include a census of housing. These questions came as the nation was recovering from the Great Depression.

Sampling, used in some subsequent censuses, means that some respondents answered a longer, more detailed set of questions than other people. Someday, future researchers will be delighted to find their folks were among the "sampled" because more information will be available about them.

You probably remember answering the census questions in 2010. A paper form was mailed to your house. Did you think of making a copy of that form before you sent it in? Remember to do that when the census for 2020 comes around. Put the copy in with your collection of personal papers so when your descendants start a search of home and family sources, they'll have a head start on census research about you, and they won't have to wait seventy-two years.

PROBLEMS WITH CENSUS RECORDS

There are some general problems with census records. Spelling is probably the primary problem, compounded by handwriting difficulties. Today, spelling is set in stone; there's usually only one correct spelling of someone's name. That's because most of us are literate, and we've been told spelling counts. Well, in the old days, spelling *didn't* count. Not only did people change the spelling of their names, other folks did it for them, too. Census enumerators were no exception. Whatever they could misspell (or spell in an alternate form), they did. Badly. Hughes could be Hewes, Moffitt might be Mawfit, Canard could go as far afield as Kinniart. Same people, same names, different spelling.

Whether you're using an index or reading the census schedules themselves, you must train your eyes to look for people, not names. If you're in doubt about the spelling of a name you find in the records, pronounce it aloud. Start a misspelling collection of your ancestors' names.

Handwriting can give you some grief. When you're working with census records, take some time to study the handwriting in the segment of the schedules you're interested in. Look for familiar first names—Sarah, Elizabeth, Laura, William, Robert, John, etc.—and study the letter forms in those words you know. They'll help you with the letters in unfamiliar names. Capital letter forms are especially troublesome. Again, find words you know in the same handwriting and note how the letters are formed. *L* and *S*, *F* and *T*, *I* and *J* can be easily confused. Penmanship classes used to teach old letter forms that we don't use anymore. The one that troubles beginning researchers the most seems to be the double "s." When two lower-case "s" letters were written together, the first might be written as a "long s." A "long s" looked like an "f" or a "p," but the loops were turned differently.

"Jesse" comes out as "Jeppe" or "Jeffe," "Missouri" looks like "Mifsouri," "Ross" is rendered "Rofs" or "Rops." One article told about a Russell family changing their name to Ruffle for a decade. No, they didn't.

Abbreviations can create confusion, too. "Wm." for William, "Jos." for Joseph, and "Jno." for John are just a few. To add to your troubles, that "m" in "Wm." or the "os" in "Jos." were sometimes raised a bit about the base line, with perhaps a little dash line underneath them. When you're copying information from the census reports and run into these little quirks, copy just what you find in the record. That "Jos." you transcribed as "Joseph" may actually have been "Jas." for James.

There are other problems with the census as well. You have no guarantee everyone told the absolute truth to the marshal who appeared at the door asking such questions as how many convicts, idiots, and paupers were in the home. You don't know which family member answered the questions. (Imagine your teenager answering the census questions.) Ages listed may be estimates. Watch for ages that end in zero—40, 50, 60—they may represent someone's best guess instead of an exact age.

Census instructions in 1850 directed the marshals to personally inquire at every residence, "and not otherwise," which meant in previous years they'd probably used other methods. You can't be sure all the instructions were followed. The information in the schedules was supposed to be given as though the questions had been asked on the official date of the census. Often, the inquiry done was weeks or months afterward. Babies born after the official date were supposed to be omitted, and people who had died since the official date were supposed to be listed as though living. It must have been confusing to all involved.

One of the most distressing problems you'll encounter is missing census records. Some of the schedules didn't survive. All or parts of census records for a particular state may be missing. And even in the surviving records, faded handwriting or poor microfilming may render the pages illegible.

At some point when you're reading census returns, you'll begin to wonder what instructions were given to the people who asked the questions. The Minnesota Population Center has devoted a section of its website <usa.ipums.org/usa/voliii/tQuestions.shtml> to answering that.

Census records are based on state and county boundaries. And those borders may not be today what they were yesterday. United States history is about acquisition of land. New territories and states were added. County boundaries changed as more people moved into a region. The best source for learning about boundary changes is William Thorndale and William Dollarhide's *Map Guide to the US Federal Censuses, 1790–1920*. There's an online version of the county boundary changes at <n2genealogy.com/maps.html>.

LOCATING COPIES OF CENSUS RECORDS

The original population schedules of the federal censuses are in the custody of the National Archives. All have been microfilmed and made available through microfilm publications. Many libraries have purchased census records in microfilm form.

The best way to use census records, however, is online in digital form. Several companies have digitized and indexed census records, and made them available either free or on a subscription basis. Even libraries with extensive census microfilm collections often subscribe to online census sources because they're so much more efficient to use than microfilm.

To use census records, you must have an idea about the time period your ancestors lived in a particular place. When you questioned your living relatives, you asked about where the family lived and who the family members were. This information can lead you to the right census reports. A case study in this chapter of census research on the Cates family illustrates the way you might approach census research.

The Family History Library in Salt Lake City has copies of census records for the entire United States. On its website, FamilySearch.org, you can search indexes to all U.S. census records and digitized images for many years (with the rest being added).

Ancestry.com offers census indexes and images of all available census records through their subscription service. Access to the transcribed 1880 U.S. census data is free (but not the digital record images).

HeritageQuestOnline <heritagequestonline.com> offers free access to census records, and the site includes images as well as indexes. (Note that the indexes cover heads of household only, not every name.) Access is through library portals—you have to log on to a participating library's website, click on the HeritageQuestOnline link, and sometimes enter a library card number.

Depending on the census year and location, many groups have posted indexes, transcriptions, and images of census records for limited areas. Do an Internet search on "Randolph County, North Carolina, census records" for example, to turn up those kinds of resources.

Start with the most recent census available and find your folks. Work backward, one census year at a time, locating family members first as adults, then as children, then the parents as children, and so on.

CENSUS INDEXES

Spelling is the biggest challenge census researchers encounter. Most census information was gathered orally. What the enumerator heard was committed to writing after it filtered through his head. That is, assuming he was given correct information to start with. See the huge potential for error there? Even if the names were written correctly, the enumerator's handwriting may be difficult to read. Or it may have been easy enough to read, but written in what seems like disappearing ink. Or everything may have been fine until the microfilm camera operator sneezed when he turned the page your ancestor is recorded on. Oops.

Censuses were taken in enumerator order—door to door. But people didn't live in alphabetical order so finding aids had to be created. Those indexes have problems, too, in addition to the poor handwriting and bad answers already in the records.

While you may instantly recognize your ancestor's name in the original records, if the person indexing those records wasn't familiar with it, she may transcribe it as something else. Add ordinary, garden-variety typos to the mix. Bottom line? Spelling doesn't count. It's like the rules in horseshoes or nuclear war—anything close counts.

If you don't find your folks in a census index, first try an alternate index. If HeritageQuestOnline's index was a bust, go to FamilySearch.org and use that index. If you have a pretty good idea about the geographic area where your family should have been in a particular census year, you can read original census pages online, paging through a county, scanning for names. But don't just look at the last names; read the family groups for first names you know, too. If you don't find your folks in a census index and can't pinpoint a small geographic area to search, try looking up their neighbors where you have found them in a more-recent census. If your Moffitt family lived around the Mendenhalls and Vestals in the 1880 census records, look those people up in the 1870 index. Then go to the original records and see if your folks are lurking under a badly written or poorly spelled entry.

SOUNDEX INDEXES

There's another category of indexes the National Archives made available as microfilm publications. These indexes are called Soundex indexes. We don't use them anymore because the online indexes are so much easier to access. You should know about them, however, in the event you run into them in some context or another. Libraries still have these microfilmed index publications, probably housed beside their census records on microfilm. All of which are gathering dust.

In the 1930s, under the federal government's program, the Works Projects Administration (WPA), unemployed white collar workers began indexing the 1880 federal census. The Social Security program had been introduced as part of President Franklin D. Roosevelt's New Deal. Under it, workers were eligible for benefits when they reached a certain age. But many of those folks were born before birth certificates were required by law. Many didn't have birth certificates even when they were required to be filed. How were these people going to prove their ages? Indexing the census returns seemed like a partial solution.

The WPA workers didn't index all of the people listed in the population schedules of the 1880 census. They only included families with children aged ten and under. They reasoned that older people listed in 1880 wouldn't be employed in occupations covered by Social Security. Some of the index cards in the project seem to have been lost before they were filmed and occasionally cards were filed out of order. So the 1880 Soundex index isn't perfect, and it's a partial index to the households found in the census schedules.

The 1900 Soundex index to the federal census schedules is much better than the one for 1880. First of all, it is an index to every family in the schedules (or it's supposed to be, anyway). A card was made for every head of household and entries on the card list all the people within that family. Cards were made for all adults whose last names are different than the head of household. It seems to be more accurate than the one for 1880.

Just when things were looking up, the 1910 Soundex is a disappointment. First of all, it doesn't cover all the states, just the twenty-one states for which no vital records office existed at the time of the 1910 census.

There are Soundex indexes for all the states in 1920, and while the accuracy doesn't equal that of 1900, it was much better than not having an index. The 1930 Soundex indexes only include the census records for twelve Southern states.

In all the Soundex indexes, names are grouped in numerical codes derived from last names, then in alphabetical order by the first name of the head of household. If you need to learn how to code a name to find it in these indexes, reference material will be available at the library that has these indexes among their collections. There's no need to clutter up brain cells now with what will probably be useless information.

The same caution applies to this index as to any other—if you don't find the person you're looking for, it doesn't mean that person isn't listed in the census schedules themselves.

OTHER CENSUS FINDING AIDS

Census indexes aren't the only tools that will tell you where your ancestors are in census records. Any document that shows where they lived can be a pointer to their census records. Deeds, rental agreements, mortgages, insurance policies, letters, diaries, voter registration cards, marriage licenses, newspaper clippings, and a hundred other items can direct you to a specific county. The closer you can come with one of these clues to a census year for which the records are available, the better your chances are of finding your folks. City directories can be especially helpful for locating your urban-dwelling ancestors in census records.

If you don't have a clue where your folks lived in a given census year, indexes at HeritageQuest-Online, FamilySearch.org, Ancestry.com, and others that have complete databases will turn up people with the same name, but you need more information to be sure they're your relatives.

STATE AND LOCAL CENSUSES

When we think about census records, it's federal records that come to mind first. All those records are available from one source, the National Archives. But those aren't the only census records that were produced. State and local governments also conducted censuses. Sometimes, those records are more difficult to learn about and locate, so they're not checked by beginning genealogists.

Information supplied in these state and local censuses varies considerably. Some were nothing more than a head count of the residents, and don't include people's names. Others are much more helpful. For a complete list of state census records, consult Ann S. Lainhart's *State Census Records*. Ancestry.com's and FamilySearch.org's online collections encompass a growing number of these state census records.

CLUES IN THE CENSUS

When you find a census entry on one of your ancestral families, think of it as a starting place. Listen to the record, don't just read it. Here are some ideas:

In the 1910 census, if your ancestor is noted as having been a Civil War veteran, look for Union or Confederate pension records, then look for military records. Check for membership in organizations such as the United Confederate Veterans or the Grand Army of the Republic. Look for records of veterans' reunions. Often card files were kept of those attending those "good old boy" events. Check the 1890 veterans' schedules for information about your ancestor (well, provided he lived in Kentucky or a state following it in an alphabetical list).

If anything points to land ownership, go to the deed books for the county of residence and search for purchases and sales of real estate. The 1900, 1910, and 1920 censuses ask if the residence is a farm or a home, and whether it's owned outright, mortgaged, or rented. Value of real estate is one of the categories on the 1850, 1860, and 1870 censuses. Even if your ancestor was renting a farm, he may have mortgaged his tools or livestock to pay for other equipment, and that mortgage may be recorded in county records.

Value of personal property is listed in 1860 and 1870 reports. If your ancestors lived in a slave state in 1860, and if the value of their personal property is large, check tax lists, deeds, census slave schedules, newspaper ads about runaways, and probate records to learn whether they were slaveholders.

If the census shows someone in the family was a convict, look for prison records and court records. Check for newspaper accounts of the crime. Paupers in the family can lead you to poor-house ledgers or county court minutes. "Idiots" and insane people may have commitment orders in the county court minutes and institutional records. Bizarre behavior also makes the news—if Cousin Albert was in the habit of wandering around naked in public (before his trip to the state insane asylum), his behavior may have been a feature item in the local newspaper.

When the census indicates anything about marriage, it's time to look for marriage records. Census records for 1850, 1860, 1870, and 1880 ask if a couple was married "within the year," that is, during the twelve months prior to the taking of the census. 1880's reports even list the month of marriage. More recent censuses show the number of years married and often whether it was a second or third marriage for one of the parties.

Naturalization information can lead to citizenship applications and passenger arrival lists. Native or "mother" tongue data can lead you into foreign research.

Information requested about whether children had attended school within the year opens up the subject of school records. In addition, school news was often published in area newspapers.

Occupations listed in the census schedules should initiate questions about employment records and other business records. A blacksmith may have kept a ledger of his accounts. A minister may be written about in publications specific to his church. Enumerators were directed to identify the denominations of ministers. Ministerial credentials may be on file at the county courthouse.

If any members of the families you find in census records lived to be remarkably old, there may be something in the newspaper about their deaths. The censuses from 1830 on identify the most senior of citizens.

Following clues in census records is a broad subject—there are hundreds of possibilities. The point is to go beyond just reading the information about your family. Study it carefully, listen to what it's saying, and let it lead you to other records.

And don't just read the entries for your family members. Read about the neighbors. Were your folks more or less wealthy than their neighbors? Were they living in a neighborhood dominated by any particular ethnic groups? Were most of their neighbors literate? Read about the other people to develop a picture of the area. You're part of the neighborhood where you live; your ancestors were, too.

Many of these suggestions about following up on research suggest records found in courthouses—and that's the topic of our next chapter.

KEY CLUES

- The U.S. Constitution mandates census taking every ten years to ensure equal representation.
- The federal census began in 1790 and has occurred every ten years since then.
- The 1790 to 1840 census identify heads of household only. All other family members are represented by a number.
- Starting with the 1850 census, every person in a household, including nuclear family members, extended family members, boarders, and servants were listed by name.
- The 1850 and 1860 included a separate Slave Schedule to enumerate slaves.
- All but 1 percent of the population schedules for the 1890 federal census were destroyed in a fire in 1921.
- Names are often misspelled in census records and ages were often guessed.
- The best way to use census records is online in digital form. Search indexes to all U.S. census records at <www.familysearch.org>.

The Cates: A Typical Case in Census Research

Jim wanted to know about his ancestors. He questioned his mother, Margie, about what she knew about her grandparents. She remembered her grandmother's name was Lula Mae Cates Teague, and she was born in Many Springs, Missouri, on July 9, 1890. She'd visited her grave in Hickory Ridge, Arkansas, several times since her death in April 1958.

Margie remembered the names of her aunts and uncles as Julian, Henry, India, and Cora. She wasn't sure about their birth order or their ages—just that they were Lula's brothers and sisters. Margie recalled a trip to Cotton Creek Cemetery in Oregon County, Missouri, to visit the graves of Lula's parents, her great-grandparents. She had made notes about the information she found on the gravestones. The names and dates on the stones were Jefferson Davis Cates, 1861–1939, and Sarah Elizabeth Lucinda Robinson Cates, 1863–1939. When pressed further, Margie remembered the names of Sarah Elizabeth's siblings as Will, Buddy (possibly his real name was Allen, she'd been told), and Martha, who'd married a man named Cypert. Margie said she'd always been told Sarah's mother, Mulbry Melinda, was half-Indian and had come from Georgia.

Jim encouraged his mother to go through old family papers, and in an old box of her grandmother's photos, she found a list written by Lula's father, Jefferson Davis Cates, of the names and birthdates of his brothers and sisters:

Granville E. Cates, 9-10-1849
Albert C. Cates, 4-30-1851
Rosher Cursean Cates, 1-14-1853
Pleasant H. Cates, 2-12-1855
Mary E. Cates, 2-1-1858
Jefferson Davis Cates, 4-24-1861
Amanda Lusena Cates, 1-22-1864
Ephrain G. Cates, 5-5-1867

Jim copied the list into his notes but he didn't change the date format; he copied them just as they were on the list. And he made a note about his source and where he'd found it.

Jim decided his first step would be to order copies of the death certificates for Lula's parents, since they'd died well after the time when vital records began to be recorded in Missouri. The certificates were very helpful. Sarah had died in May 1939 at age 75 and her husband had followed in December of the same year. He was 78. The informant listed on both certificates was Julian Cates, one of their sons.

The death certificates gave Jim two new sets of grandparents. The parents of Jefferson Davis Cates were listed as Sack Lindsey Cates and Mulberry M. Williams. Julian didn't know where his father's parents were born. Jim immediately noticed that the information he'd gathered earlier was in conflict with that on the death certificates. Hadn't his mother said Mulberry (Mulbrey in his notes) was Sarah's mother? Sarah's parents were listed as Andy Robinson, born in Illinois, and Sallie McGhee, born in Tennessee. Had Julian been mixed up about his grandparents, or was Jim's mother's information wrong? Jim had to reserve judgment on that point until he found another source.

Jim decided to try for a marriage record for Jefferson and Sarah. He reasoned that since the birthplaces of both were listed as Oregon County, Missouri, he'd see if they were married in that county. He wrote to the Clerk of the Circuit Court and received the record, showing they were married December 17, 1879. Sarah's name on the record was "Elizabeth Roberson."

Jim decided he had enough information to venture into census records. He knew who the family members were and enough to identify the family if he found them. So he went to HeritageQuestOnline's census records through a library portal. He noticed the name index for 1930 isn't complete, so he selected the "browse" option and checked Ripley County, Missouri, the place Jefferson and Sarah's death certificates mentioned. They were there, ages 68 and 66, living in a rented home near Henry Cates and his family, Margie's "Uncle Henry."

Jim checked HeritageQuestOnline's 1920 census index for Missouri and found the Cates couple still in Ripley County. When he moved back in time to 1910, he found the Cates couple in Oregon County with daughters Lula and Cora. Also in the 1910 census, Jim found Jefferson and Sarah's children, Julian, Henry, and India. They all three were grown and living in homes of their own. Julian, age 28, was married with a three-year-old son, and lived next door to Henry, age 26, also a married man with a four-year-old daughter and a two-year-old son. Both Julian and Henry had been married five years, and both of their wives were born in Kentucky.

Jim studied the neighbors listed in 1910. Just a few houses away were two families of McGehees, possible relatives. And next door to the McGehees was the family headed by Samuel Cypert, age 68, whose wife's name was Martha. Martha Cypert was 62, and Samuel was her second marriage. She'd been married to him for 29 years, and was the mother of 10 children, seven of whom were living. Her birthplace was listed as Tennessee. Was she the "Martha who married a Cypert"?

Jim moved his census search to 1900. The Cates were listed in Job Township, Oregon County:

J.D. Cates, born April 1861, age 39, born in Missouri, parents born in Tennessee
Lizzie Cates, born Aug. 1863, age 36, born in Missouri, father born in Illinois, mother in Ala. (they'd been married 20 years, and Lizzie was the mother of 5, all living)
J.W. Cates, born Jan. 1882, age 18
H.S. Cates, born Nov. 1883, age 16
I.A. Cates, born Aug. 1887, age 12
Lula Cates, born July 1890, age 9
Cora Cates, born July 1894, age 5
(both sons and all three girls were born in Missouri)

The Cates' neighbors included the Cyperts, Robinsons, and McGehees. Jim noticed Jefferson's wife's name varied in different records. Her marriage license said "Elizabeth," this census showed "Lizzie," and her death certificate listed her as "Sarah E."

Jim's search turned up another Cates family in an adjoining township in Oregon County. The family of William C. Cates, age 34, born in Missouri, is listed. William's mother, Ava E. Cates, age 66, a widow, born in Tennessee, mother of eleven, with six living, was listed in his household. Since Jefferson didn't list a brother named William, and the name Ava was unfamiliar, Jim wondered who these "stray" Cates were?

Jim decided to search for the Cates in the 1880 census schedules. He expected to find the Cates as newlyweds, based on their marriage date. He wasn't disappointed. J.D. Cates, age 19, and his wife, Sarah E., age 17, were living in Jobe Township, next door to a family of McGehees. Jefferson's birthplace in this record is listed as Arkansas.

In 1880, in the returns for Johnson Township, Oregon County, list the following Cates families:

dwelling 38
Rozier C. Cates, age 27, born in Missouri, parents born in Tennessee
Mary A. Cates, his wife, age 20, born in Tennessee
Jefferson D. Cates, age 1, born in Missouri

dwelling 39
Sack L. Cates, age 57, born in Tennessee, parents born in North Carolina
Mulbury Cates, his wife, age 58, born in Tennessee, parents born in North Carolina
Ephrain Cates, age 13, born in Missouri
Martha Roberts, age 66, Sack's sister, born in North Carolina

dwelling 40
Albert C. Cates, age 29, born in Missouri
Francis Cates, his wife, age 30, born in Tennessee
Isaac L. Cates, age 6, born in Missouri
Pleasant Cates, age 4
Ruth E. Cates, age 1

dwelling 41
Pleasant H. Cates, age 25, born in Missouri
Melvina(?) Cates, his wife, age 17, born in Missouri

This census cleared up the discrepancy about whether the death certificate was correct about Jefferson Davis Cates's mother being Mulberry Melinda or the family information that Mulberry was Sarah's mother. She was surely Jefferson's mother. The list of siblings from the family records were nearly all present except Granville, Mary, and Amanda. If married, the girls may have been right near there, but Jim didn't know their new surnames.

Those "stray" Cates from 1900 were listed in the 1880 census of Piney Township, Oregon County:

Ava E. Cates, age 46, born in Tennessee
Masqanck(?) Cates, (female) age 17, born in Arkansas
William Cates, age 14, born in Arkansas
Parthenia Cates, age 11, born in Arkansas
Elizabeth Hill, age 76, born in Tennessee (Ava's mother)
Ephraim Cates, age 24, born in Missouri
Eliza Cates, (Ephraim's wife) age 22, born in Missouri
William Farris, (Ava's nephew) age 24, born in Missouri
Thomas L. Farris, (Ava's nephew) age 20, born in Missouri

Who were these people, Jim wondered?

In 1870, the "stray" Cates family is in Jobe Township, Oregon County:

Pinkney Cates, age 44, born in Tennessee
Evaline Cates, age 36, born in Tennessee
Thomas Cates, age 17
Ephraim Cates, age 15
Mary Cates, age 9
Rebecka Cates, age 7
William Cates, age 4
Parthenia Cates, age 1
(the children were all born in Missouri)

At least we know who the missing father in 1880 was, though Ava's name was "Evaline" in 1870. The name so badly written for the female age 17 in 1880, is probably the Rebecka of 1870. Who were these people?

Jefferson Davis Cates's family wasn't anywhere to be found in 1870. But eight houses away from the "stray" Cates family in Oregon County was this family:

Figure 8–1, 1880 Census Page: This 1880 census page was reproduced from microfilm. See figure 8–4 for a re-creation of the Cates entries.

[7-290.]

Received July 23, 1880. A.

372

Page No. 5
Supervisor's Dist. No. 2
Enumeration Dist. No. 87

Note A.—The Census Year begins June 1, 1879, and ends May 31, 1880.
Note B.—All persons will be included in the Enumeration who were living on the 1st day of June, 1880. No others will. Children BORN SINCE June 1, 1880, will be OMITTED. Members of Families who have DIED SINCE June 1, 1880, will be INCLUDED.
Note C.—Questions Nos. 13, 14, 22 and 23 are not to be asked in respect to persons under 10 years of age.

SCHEDULE 1.—Inhabitants in Johnson Township, in the County of Oregon, State of Missouri, enumerated by me on the 4th & 5th day of June, 1880.

Wm T Shaver, Enumerator.

Dwelling/Family	Name	Color	Sex	Age	Relationship	Married	Occupation	Place of Birth	Father's Birthplace	Mother's Birthplace
36 36	Roy Hicks	W	M	51			Farmer	Tenn	Tenn	Tenn
	Americy	"	F	49	wife		Keeping House	Missouri	"	Mo
	Sarah E.	"	"	25	daughter			"	"	Mo
	James T.	"	M	20	son			"	"	"
	William J.	"	"	17	"			"	"	"
	John H.	"	"	13	"			"	"	"
	Martha J.	"	F	11	daughter			"	"	"
	Rachel	"	"	8	"			"	"	"
	Caroline	"	"	5	"			"	"	"
37 37	Sharp James		M	31			Farmer	Tenn	Tenn	Tenn
	Sarah E.	"	F	30	wife		Keeping House	"	"	"
	Nancy	"	"	12	daughter			"	"	"
	Elizabeth	"	"	10	"			"	"	"
	Jno. B.	"	M	8	son			"	"	"
	Tillie	"	"	5	"			"	"	"
	Anna	"	F	3	daughter			"	"	"
	James N.	"	M	2	son			Missouri	"	"
38 38	Cates Peter C.		M	27			Farmer	Tenn		
	Mary A.	"	F	20	wife		Keeping House	Mo	Mo	Mo
	Jefferson B.	"	M	1	son			Tenn	N.C.	N.C.
39 39	Cates Jack L.		M	57			Farmer	Mo	Tenn	Tenn
	Milbury	"	F	58	wife		Keeping House	N.C.	N.C.	N.C.
	Ephraim G.	"	M	13	son			Mo	Tenn	Tenn
	Roberts Martha	"	F	66	sister					
40 40	Cates Albert G.		M	39			Farmer	Mo	Mo	Mo
	Francis	"	F	30	wife		Keeping House	Mo	"	"
	Isaac L.	"	M	6	son			"	"	"
	Pleasant	"	"	4				"	"	"
	Ruth E.	"	F	1	daughter			"	"	"
41 41	Cates Pleasant H.		M	28			Farmer	Mo	Tenn	Tenn
	Melona	"	F	17	wife		Keeping House	Michigan	Ohio	Ohio
42 42	Gordon James		M	23			Farmer	Ind.	Ind.	Ind.
	Abbie	"	F	19	wife		Keeping House	Mich.	Ohio	Ohio
	Albert	"	M	3/12	son			Mo	Ind.	Mich.
43 43	Warren Elizabeth	"	F	65			Keeping House	Tenn	Tenn	Tenn
	Allen	"	"	12	daughter			"	"	"
	Josie	"	"	9				"	"	"
44 44	Fry Isaac C.		M	35			Farmer	Mo	"	"
	Mary M.	"	F	30	wife		Keeping House	"	"	"
	Sarah J.	"	"	12	daughter			Tenn	"	"
	Daniel G.	"	M	10	son			"	"	"
	Mary D.	"	F	8	daughter			Mo	"	"
	Saxton Rhoda	"	M	17	nephew			"	Mo	Mo
45 45	Johnson Robert		M	28			Farmer	Tenn	Tenn	Tenn
	Mandy	"	F	23	wife		Keeping House	Mo	"	"
	James L.	"	M	3	son			"	"	Mo
	Sorin	"	"	5/12				"	"	"
46 46	McKinzie Reuben		M	26			Farmer	Ala	Tenn	Ala
	Francis	"	F	26	wife		Keeping House	Mo	Mo	Mo
	Paulina	"	"		daughter			Ala	"	"

Note D.—In making entries in columns 9, 10, 11, 19, 16 to 22, an affirmative mark only will be used.—thus, /, except in the case of divorced persons, column 11, when the letter "D" is to be used.
Note E.—Question No. 12 will only be asked in cases where an affirmative answer has been given either to question 10 or to question 11.
Note F.—Question No. 13 will only be asked in cases where a grateful occupation has been reported in column 13.
Note G.—In column 7 an abbreviation for the name of the month may be used, as Jan., Sept., Dec.

Page No. ___5___

Supervisor's Dist. No. ___2___

Enumeration Dist. No. ___87___

SCHEDULE 1.—Inhabitants in ___Johnson Township___, in the County of ___4th & 5th___, in the State of ___Missouri___, enumerated by me on the ___Oregon___ day of June, 1880.

Note A.—The Census Year begins June 1, 1879, and ends May 31, 1880.

Note B.— All persons will be included in the Enumeration who were living on the 1st day of June, 1880. No others will. Children BORN SINCE June 1, 1880, will be OMITTED. Members of Families who have DIED SINCE June 1, 1880, will be INCLUDED.

Note C. —Questions Nos. 13, 15, 22 and 23 are not to be asked in respect to persons under at 10 years of age.

Enumerator _____

Dwelling houses numbered in the order of visitation.	Families numbered in the order of visitation	The Name of each Person whose place of abode on 1 June 1880 was in this family.	Color – White, W; Black, B; Mulatto, Mu; Chinese, C; Indian, I	Sex-Male, M; Female, F.	Age at last birthday prior to June 1, 1880. If under 1 year, give months in fractions thus: 3/12	If born within the Census year, give the month.	Relationship of each person to the head of this family—whether wife, son, daughter, servant, boarder, or other.	Single, /	Married, /	Widowed, / Divorced, D	Birthplace	Birthplace of father	Birthplace of mother
1	2	3	4	5	6	7	8	9	10	11	24	25	26
38	38	Cates, Rozier C.	W	M	27				/		Missouri	Tenn.	Tenn.
		~ Mary A.	"	F	20		wife		/		Tenn.	"	Mo.
		~ Jefferson	"	M	1		son				Mo.	Mo.	N.C.
39	39	Cates, Sack L.	"	M	57				/		Tenn.	N.C.	Tenn.
		~ Mulbury	"	F	58		wife		/		"	Tenn.	N.C.
		~ Ephrain	"	M	13		son	/			Mo.	N.C.	Tenn.
		Roberts, Martha	"	F	66		sister			/	N.C.	N.C.	N.C.
40	40	Cates, Albert C.	"	M	29				/		Mo.	Tenn.	Tenn.
		~ Francis	"	F	30		wife		/		Tenn.	Mo.	Mo.
		~ Issac L.	"	M	6		son				Mo.	"	"
		~ Pleasant	"	M	4		son				"	"	"
		~ Ruth E.	"	F	1		daughter				"		
41	41	Cates, Pleasant H.	"	M	25				/		Tenn.	Tenn.	Tenn.
		~ Melvina	"	F	17		wife		/		Michigan	Ohio	Ohio

Andrew Robertson, age 34, born in Tennessee
Sarah Robertson, age 36, born in Alabama
Martha Robertson, age 13, born in Missouri
Mary Robertson, age 10, born in Missouri
Francis Robertson, age 8, born in Missouri
Lucinda Robertson, age 7, born in Missouri
Parlee Robertson, age 4, born in Missouri
Andrew Robertson, age 2, born in Missouri
Addie Robertson, age 1 month, born in Missouri

It was a good thing for Jim his mother remembered her grandmother's full name: Sarah Elizabeth Lucinda Robinson. He might have dismissed the 1870 census entry showing Sarah as a child named Lucinda if he hadn't know about her full name. And so far, he'd found her last name as Robinson, Roberson, and Robertson. Sarah's death certificate lists her mother's maiden name as "Sally McGhee." Sally is a nickname for Sarah, so it appeared Jim had located another generation of his ancestors on the census returns.

The Robertson's next-door neighbors in 1870 were William and Martha Sypert and the family of one William McGhee, born in Alabama.

Jim didn't find Jefferson Davis Cates's family in 1870 when J.D. would have been a nine-year-old child. He knew what the family group should have looked like from his list and previous census information. They do appear in 1860, but not in Oregon County.

The 1860 census for Texas County, Ozark Township, Missouri, lists:

S.L. Cates, age 37, born in Tennessee
M. Cates, age 38, born in Tennessee
Alexander H. Cates, age 12, born in Tennessee
Granville Cates, age 11, born in Illinois
Albert Cates, age 9, born in Missouri
Rosier C. Cates, age 7, born in Missouri
Ples. H. Cates, age 4, born in Missouri
Mary E. Cates, age 1, born in Missouri

Also in Texas County, but in Piney Township, are:

M.P. Cates, age 36, born in Tennessee
Avaline, age 37, born in Tennessee
Semantha, age 27, born in Illinois

Figure 8–3, 1870 Census Page: This 1870 census page was reproduced from microfilm. See figure 8-4 for a re-creation of the Cates entries.

Page No. 81

Inquiries numbered 7, 16, and 17 are not to be asked in respect to infants. Inquiries numbered 11, 12, 15, 16, 17, 18, and 20 are to be answered (if at all) merely by an affirmative mark, as /.

SCHEDULE 1.—Inhabitants in Jobe Township, in the County of Oregon, State of Missouri, enumerated by me on the 24 day of August, 1870.

Post Office: Alton Mo

John Price, *Ass't Marshal.*

Line	1	2	3	4	5	6	7	8	9	10	11	12	13	14	15	16	17	18	19	20
1	565	569	Gibbs G. W.	59	M	W	Farmer	400	375	Tenn									/	
2			— Libbie	32	F	W	Keeping House			—						/	/			
3			— G. W.	12	M	W	At School			Mo					/	/	/			
4			— John	2	—	—				Ark										
5	566	570	Ray George	23	—	—	Farm Labor		170	Tenn									/	
6			— Sarah	18	F	W	Keeping House			Ills						/	/			
7			— Susan	6/12	—	—				Mo			Sept							
8	567	571	Ray John	46	M	W	Farmer	300	400	Tenn							/		/	
9			— Martha	40	F	W	Keeping House			—						/	/			
10			— Mary	21	—	—				—										
11			— [illegible]	15	—	—	At School			Ark					/	/	/			
12			— John	14	M	—				Tenn					x		x			
13			— [illegible]	12	F	—	Do			Mo					/	x	/			
14			— James	8	M	—				—										
15			— Isaac	4	—	—				—										
16			— [illegible]	1	—	—				—										
17	568	572	Ray [illegible]	30	M	W	Farm Labor	30	200	Tenn						/	/		/	
18			— Amanda	30	F	W	Keeping House			Mo						/	/			
19			— Sarah	14	—	—	At School			—					/	/	/			
20			— James	12	M	—	Do			—					/	/	/			
21			— William	10	—	—				—										
22			— John	4	—	—				—										
23			— Martha	6/12	F	—				—			Aug							
24	569	573	Cates Reuben	44	M	W	Farm Labor		500	Tenn									/	
25			— Evaline	35	F	W	Keeping House			—										
26			— Thomas	17	M	—				Mo										
27			— Ephraim	15	—	—				—										
28			— Mary	9	F	—				—					/					
29			— Rebecka	7	—	—				—					/					
30			— William	4	M	—				—										
31			— Martha	1	F	—				—										
32	570	574	James Herrod	63	M	W	Farmer	1800	635	Tenn									/	
33			— Sarah	50	F	W	Keeping House			—										
34			— [illegible]	24	—	—				—										
35			— Mary	30	—	—				—										
36			— Samuel	14	M	—	At School			—					/					
37			— William	10	—	—	Do			Mo					/					
38			— Sarah	4	F	—				Mo					/					
39			[illegible]	35	M	W	Black Smith	320	200	Tenn									/	
40																				

No. of dwellings, 6 No. of white females, 18 No. of males, foreign born, ____
" " families, 6 " " colored males, ____ " " females, " " ____
" " white males, 21 " " " females, ____ " " blind, ____
No. of insane, ____

Figure 8–4, 1870 Census: These census entries were re-created from the 1870 census page shown in figure 8-3. The text of the form and of the entries is accurate.

Page No. 81

Inquiries, 7, 16, and 17 are not to be asked in respect to infants. Inquiries 11, 12, 15, 16, 17, 19, and 20 are to be answered (if at all) merely by an affirmative mark, as /.

SCHEDULE 1.—Inhabitants in ___ Jobe Township ___, in the County of ___ Oregon ___, in the State of ___ Missouri ___,

enumerated by me on the ___ 24 ___ day of ___ August ___, 1870.

Post Office ___   ___, Ass't Marshal.

Dwelling houses, numbered in the order of visitation.	Families, numbered in the order of visitation.	The name of every person whose place of abode on 1 June 1870 was in this family.	Age at last birthday prior to June 1, 1880. If under 1 year, give months in fractions thus: 3/12	Description.			Profession, Occupation, or the Trade of each person, male or female	Value of Real Estate Owned.		Place of Birth, naming State or Territory of U.S.; or the Country if of foreign birth.
				Sex—Males (M.), Females (F.)	Color-White (W), Black (B), Mulatto (M), Chinese (C), Indian (I)			Value of Real Estate.	Value of Personal Estate.	
1	2	3	4	5	6		7	8	9	10
569	573	Cates, Pinkney	44	M	W		Farm Labor		600	Tenn.
		- Evaline	36	F	/		Keeping House			/
		- Thomas	17	M	/					Mo.
		- Ephrain	15	M	/					/
		- Mary	9	F	/					/
		- Rebecka	7	F	/					/
		- William	4	M	/					/
		- Parthenia	1	F	/					/

	Education		Whether deaf, and dumb, blind, insane, or idiotic	Constitutional Relations.	
Attended school within the year.	Cannot read.	Cannot write.		Male Citizens of U.S. of 21 years of age and upwards.	Male Citizens of U.S. of 21 years of age and upwards, whose right to vote is denied or abridged on other grounds than rebellion or other crime.
15	16	17	18	19	20
				/	
/	/				
/	/				
/	/				
/	/				

If born within the year, state month (Jan., Feb., &c.) — 13
If married within the year, state month (Jan., Feb., &c.) — 14

F.M., age 9, born in Missouri	
Thomas A., age 7, born in Missouri	
Ephraim J. age 5, born in Missouri	

("Semantha's" age is definitely listed as "27" on the census, so it has to be transcribed that way, but it's probably in error.)

The 1850 Missouri census index led Jim to Madison County, Missouri:

dwelling 528
Ephraim Cates, age 71, born in North Carolina
Rebeca Cates, age 56, born in North Carolina
Martha Cates, age 27, born in North Carolina

dwelling 529
Moses P. Cates, age 25, born in Tennessee
Evaline Cates, age 18, born in Tennessee
Semancy, age 1, born in Illinois

dwelling 649
Saml L. Cates, age 28, born in Tennessee
Melbina M. Cates, age 28, born in Tennessee
Emaline Cates, age 5, born in Tennessee
Alexander M. Cates, age 3, born in Tennessee
Granville H. Gates, age 2, born in Illinois

Martha Cates, age 27, was undoubtedly the sister Martha Roberts, age 66, found in Sack L. Cates's home years later. Since she's definitely Sack's sister and she's in the home of Ephraim Cates, there are strong indications Sack and Moses Pinkney Cates may be brothers. Relationships aren't stated among family members, so it would be dangerous to guess that Ephraim might have been the father of Sack and Moses P.—he's old enough to have been their grandfather, or he may even have been their uncle.

The child "Semancy" in 1850 is probably one and the same as the "Semantha" in the 1860 census, though the age in 1860 is in error. Though Sack's name is spelled "Saml" in 1850, there's no doubt this is the correct family.

Drawing from the birthplaces of the children, it appears both the families of Moses P. Cates and Sack (Saml.) Cates were in Illinois in 1848 or 1849, and had only been there briefly before their move to Missouri. About 1847, the families had been in Tennessee.

But where are the Cates in 1840? Probably in Tennessee, but only the heads of household are

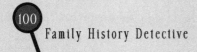

Figure 8–5, 1850 Census Page: This 1850 census page was reproduced from microfilm. See figure 8–6 for a re-creation of the Cates entries.

SCHEDULE I.—Free Inhabitants in _____ in the County of _Madison_ State of _Missouri_ enumerated by me, on the __2__ day of _Sept._ 1850. _Peter R. Peale_ Ass't Marshal.

1	2	3 The Name of every Person whose usual place of abode on the first day of June, 1850, was in this family.	4 Age	5 Sex	6 Color	7 Profession, Occupation, or Trade of each Male Person over 15 years of age.	8 Value of Real Estate owned.	9 Place of Birth, Naming the State, Territory, or Country.	10	11	12	13 Whether deaf and dumb, blind, insane, idiotic, pauper, or convict.
		Greenbard Ashlock	21	m				Tennessee			1	
		Nancy A. Ashlock	16	f				Missouri			1	
		Joseph F. Ashlock	10	m				Missouri				
		Tho? Self	7	m				Missouri			1	
522	522	Louis L. Ashlock	23	m				Tennessee				
		Selina Ashlock	19	f				Missouri				
		Sapphira Ashlock	1	m				Missouri				
523	523	John W. Miller	51	m		Farmer	3200.00	Virginia				
		John S. W. Miller	19	m				Missouri				
		Jam S. W. Miller	13	m				Missouri				
		Martha D. Miller	11	f				Missouri			1	
		James M. Miller	9	m				Missouri			1	
		Sophia L. Miller	7	f				Missouri			1	
		Julian A. Miller	5	f				Missouri			1	
		Hellen M. Miller	3	f				Missouri			1	
		Laura M. Miller	1	f				Missouri				
524	524	Geo. W. McDowel	34	m		Farmer	500.00	N. Carolina				
		Martha A. McDowel	29	f				Massachusetts				
		Geo. W. McDowel	1	m				Missouri				
		Sarah I. McDowel	16	f				Missouri			1	
525		Fayette M. Pease	27	m		Farmer		Connecticut				
		Susan A. Pease	19	f				Kentucky				
		Joseph Selly	24	m		Farmer		Tennessee				
		Sarah F. Selly	18	f				Missouri				
		Sarah E. Sell	2	f				Missouri				
		Mary I. Selly	6/12	f				Missouri				
526	526	John A. Haynes	45	m		Farmer	1000.00	Virginia			1	
		Julia Haynes	20	f				Missouri			1	
		Elvira Haynes	18	f				Missouri			1	
		Malvina Haynes	16	f				Missouri			1	
		James Haynes	14	m				Missouri			1	
		Susan Haynes	10	f				Missouri			1	
		Louisa Haynes	8	f				Missouri				
527	527	George Matlock	28	m		Farmer		Tennessee				
		Elizabeth Matlock	21	f				N. Carolina				
		James F. Matlock	5	m				Missouri				
		Snell Matlock	2	m				Missouri				
528	528	Ephraim Cates	71	m		Farmer		N. Carolina				
		Rebeca Cates	59	f				N. Carolina				
		Martha Cates	31	f				N. Carolina				

Figure 8–6, 1850 Census: These census entries were re-created from the 1850 census page shown in figure 8-5. The text of the form and of the entries is accurate.

SCHEDULE 1.—Free inhabitants in _____, in the County of ____2____, State of ___Missouri___

enumerated by me, on the _____ day of ___Sept.___, 1850. ___Peter R. Pocalo___ Ass't Marshal.

Madison

	Dwelling houses, numbered in the order of visitation.	Families, numbered in the order of visitation	The name of every Person whose usual place of abode on the first day of June, 1850, was in this family.	Age	Sex	Color (White, black or mulatto.)	Profession, Occupation, or the Trade of each Male Person over 15 years of age.	Value of Real Estate Owned	Place of Birth, naming State, Territory, or Country.	Married within the year.	Attended school within the year.	Persons over 20 y'rs of age who cannot read & write	Whether deaf and dumb, blind, insane, idiotic, pauper, or convict.
	1	2	3	4	5	6	7	8	9	10	11	12	13
1	528	528	Ephraim Cates	71	M		Farmer		N. Carolina				
2			Rebeca Cates	56	F				N. Carolina				
3			Martha Cates	27	F				N. Carolina				
4	529	529	Moses P. Cates	25	M		Farmer	$100	Tennessee				
5			Evaline Cates	18	F				Illinois				
6			Semancy Cates	1	F				Illinois				
7	649	649	Sml. L. Cates	28	M				Tennessee				
8			Melvina M. Cates	28	F				Tennessee				
9			Emaline Cates	5	F				Tennessee				
10			Alexander M. Cates	3	M				Tennessee				
11			Granville H. Cates	2	M				Illinois				

listed in the 1840 census. It's tempting for Jim to select an Ephraim Cates and decide he's the same Ephraim from Madison County, Missouri, in 1850. Jim knew he'd omitted county records. And he'd lost sight of the other people who were associated with the Cates family.

Starting in Oregon County, and moving backward in time to Texas and Madison Counties, Jim needs marriage, deed, tax, and probate records for all the members of his family, not just his direct line. He needs to investigate all the records created during the time period his family lived in those places. He needs to pay attention to people like Mrs. Hill and the Farris nephews, peripheral folks who might provide clues to help with the Cates family. Then he needs to search for the whole group of people with whom the Cates associated. They probably came from the same county in Tennessee. When he finds Ephraim Cates in Tennessee, he needs to be certain it's his Ephraim Cates, and not a man by the same name. And he needs to remember all along the way to record the sources for each piece of information so he can evaluate and analyze his findings.

YOUR DAYS IN COURT
Research at the Courthouse

The records your ancestors left behind from their day-to-day business transactions in local courthouses can be wonderfully helpful in piecing together your pedigree. When you begin to build pictures of your ancestors' lives, they become real people, not just names and dates on a pedigree chart. Deeds, wills, mortgages, marriages, probate records, court records, tax lists, and more were left in courthouses by your ancestors.

The key to getting the most from county records is knowing where your family lived so you can discover where they went to transact their business. Remember, political boundaries change over time. Consult *The Family Tree Sourcebook* by the editors of *Family Tree Magazine* and Thorndale and Dollarhide's *Map Guide for the U.S. Federal Censuses, 1790–1920* for county formation information. Use <www.n2genealogy.com/maps.html> to see the boundary changes.

When settlement began in an area, residents may have traveled many miles to the county seat, the place where local records were kept and court was held. As more people moved into that place, the residents might have petitioned the state or territorial legislature for their own, nearby county seat. Legislators listened to requests for closer, more responsive county governments, and created new counties, establishing new county boundaries. The records about establishment and adjustments of county lines are found in the session laws passed by state legislatures. Through the years, as settlement continued to grow, even more counties were formed. So your ancestors may have lived in one place, but the name of their county of residence may have changed at least once during their lifetimes.

Changing county names and boundaries can become confusing. When you locate your ancestors in a particular county, search for information about when that county was formed, the counties from which its territory was taken, and subsequent counties formed afterward. Records about your family might be in any of those jurisdictions.

County seats changed, too. As counties were formed and divided, different towns may have been selected through the years as the place where the records were kept and court was held. In a pioneer area, the first seat of county government may have been a tavern or prominent person's residence. As the county began to grow, a building devoted to county business was constructed. That building, the courthouse, contained a meeting place where court sessions were held and an office for the county clerk. As the need grew, larger and more elaborate courthouses were built.

Courthouses were subject to disasters—fires, floods, and tornadoes—just like any other building. Sometimes the disaster was on a small scale; rodents, termites, and other critters destroyed records, too. So even when you locate the right courthouse, the records you need may not have survived, but first let's talk about the kinds of records that might be available to help with your genealogical research.

While courthouses all over the United States have many elements in common, they also differ greatly. Clerks' offices are called by various names in different states. All courthouses don't contain the same kinds of records. So the information below about the records is generalized. The best policy is to learn about the records for the county where your ancestors lived. Check *Family Tree Magazine's Family Tree Sourcebook*, or use an online source such as <www.epodunk.com>.

VITAL RECORDS

When we think of vital records, the ones kept at the state level usually come to mind. But often, those are first collected at the county level, and copies of birth and death records may be in courthouses. State laws determine the collection and reporting procedures, so there are some states in which you'll find vital records at the courthouse, and others where you won't. Some county-level recording of vital information predates state vital registration, and you may find those in the county records, too.

MARRIAGE RECORDS

In most states, marriage records are kept in the county records. Laws created differences in the kinds of information collected and recorded. And those laws changed through the years. Some marriage records are just records—the minister or justice of the peace who performed the ceremony stopped by the courthouse and reported the marriages he'd performed to the county clerk. In other times and places, a license was required and the groom had to apply. Sometimes he needed a friend or

Figure 9–1, Relyea-Merrill Wedding Certificate: This certificate, complete with the signature of witnesses and the wedding party, is from a family Bible, probably the Bible given to the newlyweds as a wedding present. Unlike court records, however, this document is not acceptable as proof of marriage.

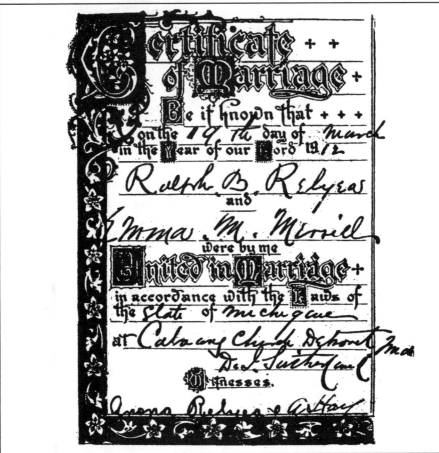

relative to sign as bondsman, guaranteeing there were no impediments to the marriage and that it would take place.

Marriage records are usually kept in chronological order. When one record volume is filled, another is started, and each covers a range of years. Each volume customarily contains an index. Sometimes the index lists both brides' and grooms' names, but frequently the index is only to the grooms' names. To find women when you don't know the names of their husbands, you must read through the marriage books themselves, scanning for brides' names.

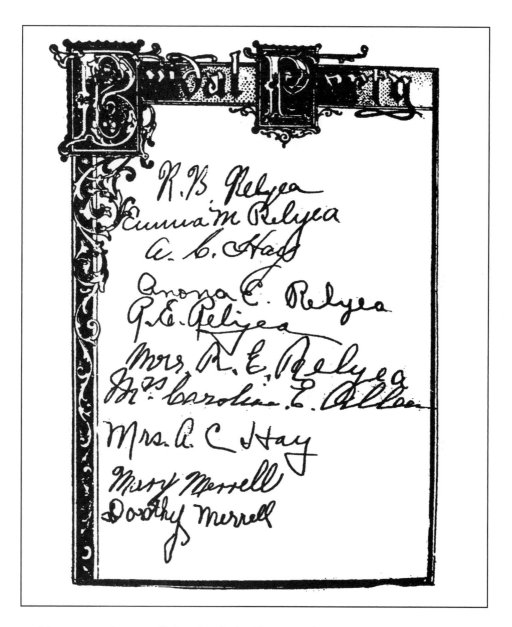

Marriage records are usually found in the bride's county of residence, and that's the first place to search. But the couple may have been married in a nearby county, and the record will appear in that county's records. Or they may have traveled to the distant home of a relative for the ceremony. If you don't locate a marriage record or license, it doesn't mean your ancestors weren't married. Always check church records and newspaper articles for marriage information.

Figure 9–2, Robertson-Dragoo Marriage Return: Although much more plain than the Relyea-Merrill certificate, this marriage return, copied from the marriage book at the courthouse in Atchison County, Missouri, constitutes legal proof of the marriage. Documents like this can often be ordered from the courthouse by mail or phone, or they may be available on microfilm through the Family History Library or the state archives.

PROBATE RECORDS

When a person died, the government, through the county courts, had an interest in seeing that person's property distributed to heirs, either according to the wishes of the deceased or in accordance with state law. If the deceased person left a will, a written document about who should inherit, it may be recorded in county records. Sometimes the will was written years before the death. When the person died, the executor, the person designated by the will to handle the estate, presented the will in court. Wills usually mention a person's children, giving genealogists links between generations.

If the deceased didn't leave a will (he or she died "intestate"), the court appointed an administrator to oversee the estate. The administrator was often the spouse or adult child of the deceased. Usually the administrator had to post an administrator's bond. Executors were required to post a bond, too, unless the wording of the will said otherwise.

The process of settling an estate created a number of records, depending upon the circumstances. If the deceased left minor children, a guardian was usually appointed to look after their interests. That person may have posted a bond to ensure any money or property was rightfully maintained. Sometimes an inventory was conducted of the deceased person's property. There may have been an estate sale, approved by the court, of the property of the deceased. Debts owed by the deceased had to be paid.

Figure 9–3, Application for Letters of Administration: Probate documents like this one name heirs and the counties and state in which they live—fuel for further investigation! Probate documents may also reveal family friends and the married names of the female members of the family.

All of the paperwork involved in the settlement of an estate was usually bundled into a packet and assigned a case file number. Short summaries of the case's progress were recorded by the clerk in large bound volumes, called "minutes" books. Case numbers are sometimes written in the margins of the minutes books, or a separate index to the case file packets may have been maintained.

Probate cases are confusing because the records are scattered in several sources. It's best to know what the law required for the time and place of the death, then make a methodical search for all the pieces of the records.

A death doesn't always result in a probate record. If a person owned less than a certain dollar amount of property (which varied according to law) when he died, no estate settlement may have been required. And sometimes, even when a settlement was required, the family may have informally divided the property and never appeared in probate court. Occasionally, an estate settlement may appear as a deed in which the potential heirs are receiving their shares of the real estate. Women

When you begin a search for court records, it's helpful to know about the court system that was in place during the time your ancestors lived in the county.

didn't have the rights they do today, and for most, there are no estate settlements separate from those of their husbands.

Some of the most informative probate cases are for childless people who owned property that had to be divided among siblings and nieces and nephews. So don't just look for records on people in your direct line—search for those collateral relatives, too.

COURT RECORDS

Probate court records, as discussed previously, are probably the most useful court records. But records from other courts can be helpful, too. Court records can be divided roughly into civil and criminal records. Criminal court records often supply information that adds to your understanding of your ancestors. But civil actions have the most potential for family historians.

If an estate settlement in probate court didn't suit one or more of the heirs, they might have sued each other, or the executor or administrator, in civil court. Other disputes among people, including divorces, often resulted in court cases. Neighbors sued over boundary disputes and water rights.

When you begin a search for court records, it's helpful to know about the court system that was in place during the time your ancestors lived in the county. A small matter may have been tried in a justice of the peace court. A civil or criminal case may have been bought in circuit court. Some states maintained a separate equity court, called chancery courts in some places, that contain a separate set of records to be searched. There are usually indexes to court cases, but sometimes the indexes don't list all the participants. It pays to look for the names of neighbors and relatives when searching court indexes.

Before 1906, naturalizations (the granting of citizenship to foreign-born people) were filed in most any court of record, including county-level courts. Those records may be found in courthouses. After 1906, naturalizations came exclusively under federal jurisdiction, and the records are found in federal court records.

DEED AND LAND RECORDS

Records about land and property transactions can be exceptionally helpful to genealogists. Deeds are legal documents that transfer title in real and personal property from one party to another. There are many different kinds of deeds, and reference works such as *Black's Law Dictionary* are helpful in learning more about deeds and other legal terms. There are several online sources for this dictionary, and the older editions are better for genealogists.

Usually the first acquisition of a parcel of land was from the government, either state or federal, and those documents conveying title are called grants or patents. They're often recorded in county deed books. Thereafter, sales are among individuals and those deeds are recorded in deed books.

The seller or grantor of a parcel of land wrote a deed conveying title to the buyer or grantee. The legal document was presented to the proper clerk of the county where the land was located where it was copied into record books. The original deed was given to the grantee, the new owner, for safekeeping.

Today, because ownership of land involves proving chain of title, deed records, even the oldest ones, are considered "working" or active records in a courthouse. Title abstractors and attorneys use them daily, so they're accessible, not stored in an attic or basement of the courthouse.

Land records can be confusing, especially the legal descriptions of the property. There are two basic divisions of states in terms of land records: state-land states and public domain states. The state-land states are the thirteen original colonies and states created from them, plus Kentucky, Tennessee, Texas, and Hawaii. The remaining thirty states are public domain states, so-called because their lands were once under the jurisdiction of the federal government.

All state-land states aren't alike in their land systems. The New England states used a "town system" in dividing parcels of land. Towns were the foundation of New England settlement, thus land records are found at three jurisdictional levels: town, county, and state.

Southern and eastern state-land states use the "metes and bounds system," or indiscriminate survey system, where legal land descriptions are based on natural features and compass bearings, and aren't tied to any larger survey. This system was useful in well-settled European countries, but when transferred to the vast wilderness of America, it had shortcomings. In addition, natural features changed over time, leading to boundary disputes.

When the American Revolution was over and Congress turned its attention to public lands, they authorized a survey system that divided the land into thirty-six square mile townships. In an area to be surveyed, a meridian line was run north and south. Baselines were established, running east and west. A grid of survey lines was imposed on the land so precise descriptions could be written. This is known as the Rectangular Survey System.

Knowledge of the survey system for the area where your ancestors lived is essential. Without it, the deeds you find will read like mumbo-jumbo. Legal verbiage in deed records, and other records as well, can be confusing, too. A good legal dictionary will help. Query online resources for more information about survey systems.

VOTER ROLLS

Courthouses may contain lists of voters for elections held under the jurisdiction of county officials. Sometimes only current voter rolls are maintained, but old lists may exist in county records. Voter registration information may exist at city and state levels, too.

Voter rolls may seem to be of limited value, but some, depending upon time and place, contain physical descriptions, citizenship information, and occupations, in addition to residence information.

More recent voter lists may contain Social Security numbers, though privacy issues have raised concerns about that practice lately.

TAX LISTS

People have to pay for the government's operating expenses, and the records left behind in the tax collection process can be very helpful in your research. Just as tax codes today require some study to understand the rules, the old tax laws covered only some folks and certain kinds of taxable property.

The information in tax lists varies widely, depending upon time and place. In general, old tax lists contain the names of free adult males. Women are listed only in special circumstances. Sometimes a uniform head tax, or poll tax, was assessed on men of a certain age, whether or not they were property owners. Land, livestock, and slaves were taxable property. In some areas, items such as gold jewelry and pleasure carriages were taxable items.

In order to use tax lists, you must learn what the laws required for the time and place where your ancestors lived. Then you need to know what records were created in the tax collection process, and, of those, which records survive.

After you locate the records, study their arrangement. Some are compiled in initial order, grouping all surnames together that start with the same letter. Others may be arranged by land description.

If you're fortunate enough to find ancestors living in a time and place where long runs of tax records are available, search through the tax books to learn more about your family members. Were they more or less wealthy than others in the area? Do you find the names of relatives, friends, and fellow travelers whom you know associated with your family?

When a new county was created, a copy of the current tax books for the annexed area may have been created. And even though a county's records may have been destroyed, check for tax book copies sent to state offices.

In many areas, substitute census records have been created from tax lists by genealogical compilers. They aren't as complete as a real census would have been, but they make excellent resources for genealogists. Remember to read the introduction to these secondary sources very carefully for information about what was (and was not) included.

MILITARY RECORDS

Military records for most American soldiers are held at the national level. The National Archives in Washington, DC, has records of soldiers from the Revolutionary War through the Spanish-American War (1898), including those for Confederate service in the Civil War. The National Archives branch in East Point, Georgia, has draft registration records for potential World War I soldiers. Records for soldiers in wars fought during the twentieth century are housed at the National Personnel Records Center in St. Louis.

America's soldiers were of two kinds: regulars and volunteers. Regular soldiers are what we think of today as career military service people. Volunteer soldiers, even those who were drafted, are citizens called upon for service in times of war. The records for regular soldiers are filed separately from those of volunteers.

Figure 9–4, Declaration of Intention: The declaration of intention was the first step in the naturalization process. This document was found in a family photo album and proved immensely valuable to the family genealogists. They were able to search the same courthouse for further information.

States often maintained records about their soldiers in an adjutant general's office, or some other state-level agency. National and state records overlap in their scope. While most military records aren't local records, nevertheless, there are military records in local courthouses. Soldiers from World Wars I and II recorded their military discharges at their local courthouses. Depending upon time and place, militia lists sometimes exist in county records.

Besides military service records about the war experiences themselves, soldiers generated records as a result of applying for benefits. Most common were applications for pensions from the federal government. These came directly from Washington and little information about them exists in courthouses. Ex-Confederate soldiers applied for pensions from the state governments of Alabama, Arkansas, Florida, Georgia, Kentucky, Louisiana, Mississippi, Missouri, North Carolina, Oklahoma, South Carolina, Tennessee, Texas, and Virginia. They applied according to their state of residence, not their state of service. While the pensions were administered at the state level, payments to veterans and their widows were often made through county offices, generating local records.

During the Civil War, some state governments passed laws directing county officials to care for indigent widows and children of servicemen. These "indigent lists" may be found in courthouses.

Soldiers who served in wars before the Civil War applied for bounty land under the various laws passed by Congress, and records about the land they received were generated at the county level when they recorded their land acquisitions.

NATURALIZATION RECORDS

Naturalization is the granting of citizenship to people from other countries. Because settlers were welcomed in the American colonies, naturalization consisted of little more than oaths of allegiance for people coming from non-British lands. When the United States was formed, Congress began to pass laws regulating naturalization. Since 1795, aliens have been subject to a five-year process for becoming citizens. In general, an initial application or "first papers" had to be filed, followed five years later by the filing of "final papers" in any court of record. In 1906, a major change took place in the naturalization process—naturalizations then had to be filed uniformly in federal courts. Genealogists looking for naturalization records created before 1906 may find them in the papers of any court of record, including those in local courthouses.

RECORDS NOT IN THE COURTHOUSE

There are records you won't find in the county courthouse where your ancestor went to do day-to-day business. The key to figuring out which records you won't find involves a magic word: *jurisdiction*. Public records are created because of legal requirements. The level of government involved determines where the records are kept.

Think about your own life. You're touching public records at different jurisdictional levels. When you get a parking ticket, you pay it at city hall, the municipal level. Your real estate taxes are paid at the county level; automobile tags are registered at the state level; and you pay federal income tax at the national level. Your ancestors' lives touched the records at these jurisdictional levels, too, though for different purposes.

Just as all the records about you aren't at your local courthouse, the records about your ancestors aren't either. If your ancestor's lawsuit against a neighbor was appealed to a higher court, the records may be in state jurisdiction. The land your ancestor acquired directly from the federal government has a land entry case file in Washington, DC, at the national level. Military records, as noted above, are usually federal records.

Private records are another category of materials you don't routinely find in courthouses. Newspapers, created by commercial publishers, are not public records. They do, however, contain information about courthouse business: news accounts of trials, land office notices, lists of delinquent taxpayers, estate settlement notices, and other legal announcements. The best place to find newspapers is in libraries and archives.

Church records aren't public records, either. Ministers registered their credentials with the county clerks, and churches sometimes recorded their charters in county record books. Deeds for church property and cemeteries managed by churches are recorded in county deed books just like other land transactions. If some church matter resulted in a lawsuit, there will be public records about the case. But other than these kinds of matters, church records are private, not public records.

BEFORE YOU GO TO THE COURTHOUSE

Once you find the right county to search for records, your next step isn't to speed off to that courthouse. Of course, if it's nearby and convenient, do jump in your car and go. Chances are, however, the places your ancestors lived are far removed from your residence. The best way to start your research in county records is to visit a local FamilySearch Center (formerly Family History Centers). The FamilySearch.org website has location information for FamilySearch Centers. (See chapter 6.)

Many county records of interest to genealogists have been microfilmed by the LDS Church. Marriages, wills, deeds, probate minutes, court records, and tax lists are available through Family-Search Centers. Using the records is a multistep process. First you must visit a center or <www.familysearch.org> and use the library catalog (choose the place-names search option) to find out which of the records are available for the county your ancestors lived in. The microfilm is housed in the Family History Library in Salt Lake City, and you can fill out rental requests to borrow the rolls you need for a small fee. More and more of this material is being digitized and put online, but it's not all there yet. Some counties have posted records online—do a thorough Internet search to see if the records you need are online.

It's much easier to use county records in air-conditioned comfort at a FamilySearch Center than to poke around in a musty, dusty courthouse. Unfortunately, the Mormons haven't microfilmed everything. Some of the records you need may only be available by visiting in person or hiring a researcher.

You may be able to write and request copies of specific records from the appropriate clerk's office, but don't expect courthouse employees to do research for you. Some county officials don't answer out-of-state requests at all. Others pass genealogy letters along to local people who do research for a fee.

Before you jump in your car, do a little preparation first. Write or call the county courthouse to be absolutely certain the records you need are available. Don't assume records created at the county level will still be at the courthouse—they may have been transferred to an archival facility. Or they may be stored in a warehouse and require an advance appointment so they can be retrieved. The courthouse may be closed for asbestos abatement or some obscure state holiday. On a not-so-obscure holiday, a researcher headed for a courthouse drove halfway across the state of Oklahoma only to learn Columbus Day was a holiday there, too. Local fair parades often close courthouses. And the days just before and after elections are a really bad time to visit.

VISITING A COURTHOUSE

Anytime you do something new, you have to learn a few rules and a bit about how to conduct yourself. It's no different when you visit records repositories.

**Harrison County Public Library
Elizabeth Branch**

"Justis of the Peas"

Courthouse research is tough, but the payoffs can be extraordinary. Here's a true story in a fellow researcher's words that supplies some inspiration on this topic. The names have been changed—this could be your family line. The connecting clue you need could be in a dusty file in a courthouse.

"It didn't take me long to realize that no matter what name I chase, there are at least two men of the same name, and only one of them is mine. Bravely, I waded into the William Freemans of New York state, one of whom had to be my ancestor who had migrated on to Michigan. Looking carefully at each, I began crossing them off my list of possibilities.

"It couldn't be the William in Westchester County—he was still on the census after my William had gone west. It wasn't the William in Broome County, because his census record only listed half the number of children mine could boast. Not William in Saratoga County; I found a cemetery listing for him in a book at the library. I tossed out the W.T. in Oneida County and the William R. in Monroe County as well—they were simply the wrong ages. The William "Treeman" who lived in Onondaga County was a tempting prospect because he did move to Michigan. I found a will for him with a bequest to a sister back in Onondaga County, but the names of his children mentioned in the will didn't match the names in my family.

"I was down to two men of the name—one in Cayuga County, the other in Genesee County. It was time for a courthouse trip. I marshaled my forces and put together everything I knew about my ancestor. I took information from his tombstone, the names and years of birth of this children from the census, and a copy of his will which named those children. I even studied his neighbors in Michigan with the idea that some of them might be long-time buddies who had lived near him back home. I hopped into my car and drove off in a fog of ancestral hopes.

"My first stop was the courthouse in Genesee County. There was nothing there to connect that William to my family. I was down to my last option, the William in Cayuga County. I was still green at the courthouse business, but I tried to follow all the rules. I arrived early in the day, nicely dressed, and I inquired politely, waited patiently for record books, and even refrained from telling the clerk my ancestor's life story.

"My efforts didn't appear to be working—it didn't seem to me the court minute books, deeds, and tax lists were helping me decide if this was my particular William Freeman. In desperation, since it was now nearing the end of a long and fruitless day, I asked if there were other records I could see. I was trundled off to a dusty storeroom in the basement where I could examine the original case files of the county court.

"The court minutes mentioned a case in which a William Freeman was a witness, so I began to comb the storage boxes for a packet with that case number on the outside. The clock was racing. Fifteen minutes to five, and I finally found it. Folded up inside the packet were a number of small, irregularly shaped pieces of paper: a deposition from the plaintiff stating his view of the case, the judge's order releasing the disputed wagon to the victorious party, a yellowed newspaper clipping announcing the hearing in a legal notices column, and finally the report of a preliminary hearing in a justice of the peace court that had dissolved into a fist fight.

"What? I blinked, and blinked again. There at the bottom of that report was the signature of the official, 'Wm. Freeman, Justis of the Peas.' Loop for loop, letter for letter, the signature matched the one on the will in my file folder. I'd found my ancestor. I left the courthouse with a huge smile. That William Freeman of Cayuga County couldn't spell very well, but he was mine, all mine."

Remember your manners. Please and thank you go a long way with nearly anyone, including courthouse staff. And they'll have more respect for you if they can tell you've done your homework in advance and know what you're looking for. Keep your requests brief and leave off the fascinating stories about your ancestors.

Wear business attire instead of your party-animal T-shirt and shorts. Yes, you're on vacation and perfectly within your rights to dress casually, but if you'll slip into a phone booth (well, maybe not a phone booth) and change into your Super-Researcher costume, you'll command a little more respect and attention from the staff. If you can't bear the thought of a tie or panty hose, pretend it's a costume party, and wear one or the other anyway. Leave your children, uninterested spouse, and pets elsewhere.

Photocopies may be expensive. Some of the record volumes you use may be too large or fragile to photocopy at all. Digital cameras come in handy here. Be prepared to take notes. Remember to use a research calendar and list all the sources you search, including the ones that weren't productive. An easy way to keep track of the record books you've used is to photograph the spines as you go.

While you're searching, be sure to stay tuned in for the names of neighbors and associates of your ancestors. Notice who witnesses deeds and serves as bondsmen for your family members. Make a note of the ministers who perform marriage ceremonies for your folks. In the record books, look well beyond the time you know your family lived in the area. Sometimes deeds weren't recorded until many years after they were actually signed. Estate settlements may not have been finalized until the youngest heir was of legal age. Don't just raid the records for names; study them carefully and listen to what they're telling you about your ancestors' lives.

Ask courthouse staff members for the names of local people who spend time poking around in their records. You may discover an expert who can help with your research.

Above all, remember to express your appreciation for the help you receive. A fruit basket or box of candy is appropriate for staff members who were especially kind and helpful.

KEY CLUES

- Courthouse records can be wonderfully helpful to genealogists. Arm yourself with information about local history, knowledge of the structure of local records, and an understanding of the land survey system before you wade into the records. Think of yourself as a detective—courthouses hold the answers to many mysteries.

PUTTING IT ALL TOGETHER
Sharing Your Family History

You've tramped through countless cemeteries, talked to dozens of relatives, visited lots of courthouses, haunted scores of libraries and archives, and read countless books about history and research methodology. What's next? You didn't fill out all those family group sheets and enter all that computer data just for yourself, did you? It's time to share it with your nuclear family, extended family, and distant genealogy cousins. After you've been through the genealogy learning process, it's time to share general information about what you've learned with others who are just starting their family history research.

Genealogy can be a great way to pull your family closer together. Involve your spouse and children and turn this pursuit into a family affair. Plan family vacations around your research needs. Surely there's a water theme park along the route to a courthouse you want to visit. Contact the Chamber of Commerce or tourism office for the areas you're interested in and ask about accommodations and attractions. One-half of the parent partnership can take the kids on a walking tour of the historic district while the other does research in the courthouse or library. Remember not to inflict your small children on the courthouse staff or librarian, but do take them to cemeteries and museums.

Use genealogy as a way to put your children in touch with grandparents, aunts and uncles, and cousins who live in faraway places. Encourage them to write letters and send e-mail messages to relatives. They can share drawings, photos, and stories about day-to-day events.

Involving your children in the research process will not only give them a sense of their heritage and ancestors, it can sharpen investigative and reasoning skills they can use in other areas of their lives. Let them develop map-reading and geography skills as you share what you've learned about your ancestors.

ORGANIZING A FAMILY REUNION

Participating in a family reunion is a way to share your information with family members outside your nuclear family, and learn more at the same time. If your family holds an annual reunion, be sure to get involved. As you talk with distant members of the family, ask if they hold reunions. Make plans to attend. Many families schedule get-togethers on Memorial Day, Independence Day, and Labor Day.

Family reunions can be small-scale affairs where all the brothers and sisters of a particular couple gather and bring their offspring for a big family meal. Or they can involve hundreds of people descended from a common ancestor of the Colonial period congregating from all over the country and spending a weekend at a resort.

If your family doesn't have an ongoing reunion, you can start one. First, call a meeting of your relatives who have expressed an interest in gathering the family together. You can meet in person, with a conference telephone call, or online through business-meeting software. Form a reunion committee. Pool your address books and contact lists to make a roster of all your relatives on that family line. The committee member with organizational skills can be appointed the list manager; the member who lives in the area where the reunion will be held can be the local arrangements manager; someone with creative ideas can be the entertainment manager. Your cousin with artistic talent can design announcement flyers. Other responsibilities can be meted out according to talents and interests.

Decide on a time and place for the event. Start planning early so vacation time can be reserved by those family members who are gainfully employed. Some employers require employees to make vacation time reservations around the first of the year. No date will suit everyone; there will always be people who have prior commitments.

Select a place for the event. An ancestral hometown or city convenient for many family members is a good choice. Look for a park pavilion, community meeting room, or some other public meeting place that can be reserved in advance. Be sure to pick one with adequate space for the number of folks who'll attend. And no place will suit everyone. Do try to select one with hotel facilities in the area; it isn't fair to descend on one cousin's home.

Notify everyone on your mailing list about the reunion as soon as you have set the date and place. Ask them to respond to your announcement letter with the addresses of more cousins who might be interested. Plan on mailing, on paper or electronically, at least two flyers—one early, and the other a few weeks before the reunion. Ask attendees for money to defray the cost of out-of-pocket expenses and renting a site for the event. Suggest that each person make a small contribution. Keep track of the money—how much was received and where it went—in case someone asks. Advertise your reunion in area newspapers and online sites.

Encourage everyone to bring photograph albums to share with others. Plan special activities but leave unstructured time for visiting. Consider awarding inexpensive prizes or certificates for the oldest and youngest people in attendance, the person who traveled the longest distance to attend, the baldest, the tallest, the couple married the longest time, the most newly-wed couple, and other categories. You might conduct a search for the person at the reunion who most resembles a photo of great-grandfather. Line up the contestants, then have family members vote with their applause.

Encourage your reunion committee members to plan activities that will entertain and tie the family together. Organize tours of the local cemeteries where family members are buried.

Encourage your reunion committee members to plan activities that will entertain and tie the family together. Organize tours of the local cemeteries where family members are buried.

Make a wall-size display of the family tree and let people write their names on paper leaves and pin them on the tree. Be sure everyone at the reunion has on a name tag large enough to be read in photographs taken at the reunion. Appoint a camera person and reporter to create video interviews with family members. Show the video of last year's reunion.

Plan ahead for the meals involved, and be sure the burden doesn't fall too heavily on one or two family members. Consider a pot-luck supper if most family members are within driving distance. If you're holding the reunion in a hotel's meeting rooms, talk with the banquet staff about setting up a special buffet for your group. When planning your meals, consider special dietary requirements for health and religious reasons.

Use the reunion event itself as a research laboratory—question family members about births, marriages, and deaths in their branches. Ask about career and school accomplishments. Note new phone numbers and addresses. Record variations on family stories that have come down through other branches of the family.

Perhaps you can share the information you've already found in your research. Consider compiling a book about your findings. Start early on this project; it will take more time than you think.

PUBLISHING YOUR FAMILY HISTORY ONLINE

You can publish your family history online. Set up an Internet home page, or a Facebook account devoted to a particular ancestor (do this with Facebook's "Groups" option). Create a blog about your research and add photos, information, and documents as you turn them up.

The biggest advantage to online distribution of your information is that it can easily be kept up-to-date. New discoveries can instantly be posted to your website, blog, or Facebook page. People researching your ancestors can readily find material you've posted online. It's as close as a Google search.

For all its advantages, online publication isn't the ultimate solution. There's still a need for well-researched, carefully written family histories preserved in traditional book format.

WRITING YOUR FAMILY HISTORY

Even though you've shared information through online sites, at some point you should consider writing your family history.

If you feel disorganized, go back and reread the chapter on keeping records. Arranging your findings gives you another chance to analyze and evaluate what you've turned up.

Don't wait to "finish" your research—genealogy doesn't end (every ancestor has two parents); all you can do is choose convenient stopping places. Perhaps you've reached a point where you must make a research trip to find more information, but you can't leave career and family responsibilities to go. Call a halt for the time being and write about your findings. Maybe the records are available to you, but they just don't answer your questions about the links between the generations. Possibly a family reunion is coming up and you want to share your findings with your cousins. It's time to write.

If you've been entering data into a computer program, you can experiment with the report functions to print out your information in a variety of ways. But a genealogy is more than just a list of your ancestors; it's the story of those folks, too. Include legends and tales you've heard, and interesting tidbits you've turned up in your research. Write about problems you've encountered. If you can't identify an ancestor's parents, say so. And say why. Perhaps someone else will take up your work in coming years and solve the problem.

Arrange your information in some kind of logical order. The best choice is often to pick an ancestral couple and write about them and their descendants. Patricia Law Hatcher's book *Producing a Quality Family History* can be of tremendous assistance. It tells you how to organize and arrange your findings, and how to present them in a logical, well-structured order.

If you're using a computer program to manage your genealogy information, it will help you print out your findings. But don't be tempted to print out a series of family group sheets as a substitute for a correctly numbered family history.

When you write about your family, stick to the facts. Let them speak for themselves. Don't be tempted to make up dialogue or interject what you think their motives might have been. Write about what you've found in the records, and what you think it means, and be sure your readers can tell the difference. Collect photos and documents and draw maps and diagrams to supplement your story.

Remember the previous admonitions in this book about writing source citations for every bit of evidence you gather? You'll need those citations now. When you write your family history, you

When you write your family history, you want your family members to admire and respect your words. They'll do that more readily if you supply the information about how you know what you know.

want your family members to admire and respect your words. They'll do that more readily if you supply the information about how you know what you know.

There is another reason to add citations to your work: to give credit where credit is due. People's words may be copyrighted, depending upon the sources you use. Proper attribution with use of a small segment of a published work (we're talking a paragraph or two) probably lets you off the hook for a copyright infringement suit. If there's doubt in your mind about how much of someone else's words is too much, you should contact the author and ask for permission. The flip side of that coin is that you don't want credit for someone else's mistake. Say where you got your information!

PUBLISHING YOUR FAMILY HISTORY

The best way to preserve your family history is to print traditional books and distribute copies. Yes, the information you've published online is a wonderful idea, but think long-term and put a real book together.

Publication of your family history can be as simple as taking your camera-ready pages to a local photocopy shop and having several copies made. ("Camera-ready" means the printed pages will look just like the ones you've prepared on your computer.) Add cardstock covers, choose a binding option, and you can have inexpensive books to share with your family members. If you need less than one hundred copies of your book, the photocopy method is probably the most economical choice.

For larger print runs, you might consider commercial printers who specialize in family histories. These companies aren't publishers—they don't market or advertise your book. Be careful to investigate carefully before you select a printer. Beware of anyone who claims there are profits to be made on family histories; the profits they're referring to are their profits, made at your expense. Prices per-book decrease as you increase the number of copies you have produced at one time by a commercial printer. The ideal number of books to have printed is enough so that you won't have to immediately reprint the book, but not so many that they sit unsold in your garage for years to come.

Another option for publication of your family history is photo-book publishers. Blurb.com prints books with black and white text pages as well as color photo pages. The responsibility for writing, designing, and laying out the book is all yours, though there are many tutorials at Blurb.com to help you. Once created, your book can be made available to people who want to order copies. You can establish a retail price higher than publication costs and realize a profit on sales. The advantage is no out-of-pocket publication money. Lulu.com offers a similar service.

Ancestry.com's website is connected to the photo book publisher MyPublisher.com. You can create family histories with color photos and documents from data you've posted on Ancestry.com. Those books can be shared with relatives with options to purchase their own copies.

DISTRIBUTING COPIES OF YOUR FAMILY HISTORY

Some genealogists give away copies of their family history publications, but most people can't afford to do that on a large scale. Many family histories are sold for a price that covers printing costs and advertising fees, but genealogists rarely recover the cost of the research that went into the book's production. It's a labor of love, and even at that, it's difficult to sell family members a fifty-dollar book.

As a beginning genealogist, keep the idea in mind that you'll probably want to share your research results at some time in the future. Gather the names and mailing addresses (snail mail and e-mail) of everyone you talk with about your family—they're potential buyers of your book. Start a separate address book and contact list for your genealogy cousins. Be sure to note how they're related to you. Some genealogy computer programs offer an address-book feature to help you manage these contacts.

When you publish a family history, send an announcement to everyone connected to the family line you've written about. This sale flyer or brochure should describe the book in detail, state the price and postage costs, and encourage purchase of the book. Some authors of genealogy books do this before they actually commission the printing, in order to determine the number of copies in the press run. This is called a prepublication sale and the flyer and other promotional material should state very clearly the anticipated shipping date for the book. And that date should have a margin for delay built into it. If you use an online service such as Blurb.com or Lulu.com, you can send links about your book to people by supplying their e-mail addresses.

Use the small profits you make from the sale of your book to supply copies of it to libraries. Give a copy to the Family History Library in Salt Lake City. Give one to your local library and to the libraries in the areas where your ancestors lived. Give one to the largest genealogical library in your state. These copies you donate to libraries will ensure that your book will live on.

> Many family histories are sold for a price that covers printing costs and advertising fees, but genealogists rarely recover the cost of the research that went into the book's production. It's a labor of love.

JOINING GENEALOGICAL SOCIETIES

So far, we've talked about sharing your genealogy research results with your family members. Beginning genealogists think of family members as familiar faces. With more research, they discover distant cousins. Finally, they see the whole world as a giant network of related people. We're all cousins. Genealogists are those folks who know how we're all related.

And all of us like being among people who share our interests. Join a genealogical society in your area. It's fun being able to get excited about a death certificate among folks who understand. Enjoy the friendship of people who feel your passion. Learn from others who've already cleared the research hurdles you're facing.

Most genealogical societies offer regular meetings and some kind of periodical. Some are entirely devoted to genealogy; others go under the banner of historical societies. Some focus on a particular county, others are statewide in focus, still others are ethnic-group specific. Join a group in your local area, even if you have no roots there. Remember the adage, "what goes around, comes around"? It's true in genealogy, too. If you join your local group, even though you have no ties to the area, and help with records restoration projects and cemetery inventories, someone in the place where your ancestors lived will do the same.

Consider joining the local society where your ancestors lived, even though it's a long-distance membership. You probably can't attend the meetings, but you'll benefit from their periodical and they'll gain your financial support.

> Don't just join genealogy groups—participate in them. Get involved.

To find a group in your area, call your local library and ask for the name of a contact person with a genealogy or historical society. Or check newspapers' lists of upcoming meetings. Look online for information about genealogy groups. After you've found the group, ask for membership information and sit in on a regular meeting or two. Visitors are always welcome. Watch for announcements about special genealogical workshops and seminars.

Don't just join genealogy groups—participate in them. Get involved. Genealogy societies run on volunteer effort. Share your information. Share with family, near and far. Share with other researchers. And share yourself with genealogical and historical groups.

You can design a self-education program that will help you with your genealogy research. Continuing education departments of local schools and colleges often offer genealogy classes. Be a wise consumer—contact people who've taken a previous class from the same instructor and ask how they feel about their learning experience. The kind of learning that can assist your genealogical endeavors isn't limited to genealogy workshops and classes. Sign up for a title abstracting course offered to real estate agents so you can learn how to read deeds. Take a course on surveying. Enroll in a nonfiction writing class. Sign up for computer classes. Take a class on effective communication skills. Look online for classes that will help you be a better family historian.

THE BOTTOM LINE

You started this search for information because you wanted to know who you are. Follow the suggestions in this book and you'll learn about your ancestors, that marvelous group of people who contributed to your gene pool, who had an impact on who you are.

Genealogy is exciting! It's so personal—a journey of self-discovery. When you read court records about your great-grandfather's fits of temper, perhaps you'll better understand where those little tantrums come from in your close family members. When you feel an urge to pull up stakes and take a job in some distant state, you'll know your ancestors had itchy feet, too.

Don't keep this hobby to yourself. Encourage your other close family members, friends, neighbors, and relatives to search for their ancestors, too. We're all part of a global community. We're all cousins.

KEY CLUES

- Involve children in your research process to give them a sense of their heritage and ancestors as well as sharpen their investigative and reasoning skills.
- Use family reunions as a way to share your discoveries with extended family members, conduct interviews, and share family photos.
- Publish your research in a blog or on a social media site such as Facebook.
- Join a local genealogy society where your ancestor lived, even if it is a long-distance membership. You'll benefit by receiving the societies periodicals.

APPENDIX A

GUIDE FOR SOURCE CITATIONS

The purpose of this basic guide to source citations is to take the mystery out of writing information about how you know what you know. Don't worry about the commas and periods; they'll vary according to different guides anyway. But do read the examples to learn what you need to record about the material in which you find information about your ancestors.

The examples given are for footnote listings; bibliographic entries will be different in their structure. If you have enough information to write a footnote for your family group sheet, you'll have enough to write the bibliographic entry when you get around to compiling your family history.

When you begin to write a source citation, think about the readers who will come after you. Could they take the information you've supplied and easily find the material again? It's better to write too much about a source than too little.

Source	Footnote Example
Article	Morton Gitelman, "The First Chancery Court in Arkansas," *The Arkansas Historical Quarterly* 55 (Winter 1996): 357–382.
Bible Record (attempt to list provenance; that is, say who the Bible has belonged to in previous years)	Family data, Robert Harmon Williams Family Bible, *The Holy Bible Containing the Old and New Testaments* (New York, n.p., 1890); original owned in 1997 by Desmond Walls Allen. The Bible was passed from Robert H. Williams to his son, Curtis H. Williams, and by Curtis to his great-niece, Desmond.
Birth Certificate (state issued)	Hadley Edward Hirrill, birth certificate no. 103-81-001272 (1981), Arkansas Department of Health, Division of Vital Records, Little Rock.
Book	Jane Gray Buchanan, *Thomas Thompson and Ann Finney of Colonial Pennsylvania and North Carolina* (Oak Ridge, Tenn.: privately printed, 1987), 238–259.
CD	Desmond Walls Allen, *Pence Funeral Home, Conway, Arkansas, 1881–1945, Three Volumes on CD,* (Conway, Ark.: Arkansas Research, Inc., 2007), Hezekiah Jones listing.
Cemetery Marker (secondary source)	Wanda M. Newberry Gray, *Cemeteries of Sebastian County, Arkansas*, Vol. 1 (Fort Smith, Ark.: privately published, 1997) 47 (Evans Cemetery).
Cemetery Marker (original stone)	Harrison Williams' tombstone, Herpel Cemetery, Stone County, Arkansas (5 miles east of Mountain View at Herpel); photographed by Thurlow Williams, 1988.

Source	Footnote Example
Census, Federal, 1790–1840 (microfilmed)	Maryann Hightower household, 1840 U.S. census, Izard County, Arkansas, p. 196, line 15; National Archives microfilm publication M704, roll 18.
Census, Federal, 1850–1870 (microfilmed)	Nathan Moffitt household, 1850 U.S. census, Lawrence County, Arkansas, population schedule, Strawberry township, p. 310, dwelling 428, family 437, National Archives microfilm publication M432, roll 27.
Census, Federal, 1880–1930 (microfilmed)	Jonathan Jones household, 1880 U.S. Federal census, Faulkner County, Arkansas, population schedule, Cadron township, enumeration district 42, supervisor's district 1, sheet 12, dwelling 223, family 228, National Archives microfilm publication T9, roll 43.
Census, Federal, Ancestry. com (from online database)	Nathan Moffitt household, Source Citation: Year: *1850*; Census Place: *Strawberry, Lawrence,* Arkansas; Roll: *M432_27*; Page: *221A*; Image: *446.* Source Information: Ancestry.com. *1850 United States Federal Census* [database online]. Provo, UT, USA: Ancestry.com Operations, Inc., 2009. Images reproduced by FamilySearch. Original data: Seventh Census of the United States, 1850; (National Archives Microfilm Publication M432, 1009 rolls); Records of the Bureau of the Census, Record Group 29; National Archives, Washington, D.C.
Church Record	David Grimes admitted to membership, 2 October 1889, Record Book 2, 1888–1893, p. 27, St. James Methodist Church, Stone County, Arkansas, Hendrix College Library, Conway, Arkansas.
Death Certificate, State	Catherine E. Makepeace, death certificate no. A376 (1925), Washington State Board of Health, Olympia.
E-mail Message	Patsy Pope, "Our Family," E-mail message from ppope1943@netscape.net to Desmond Walls Allen, 16 January 2011.
Family Group Sheet	Desmond Walls Allen, "Tyre Martin Lingo – Martha Catherine Anderson family group sheet," supplied 15 January 2005 by Desmond to Shirley Walls Manual.
Image File (electronic photograph file)	Photo: James Henry Walls, about 1864, probably Texas County, Missouri. Image file gpawalls.jpg scanned by Rob Walls, 123 Main, Sunnyvale, Calif., 12 February 2006, from original photo in his possession.
Deed	John Lancaster to Peter Mitchell, Izard County Deed Book H, p. 274, County Clerk's Office, Courthouse, Melbourne, Arkansas.

Source	Footnote Example
Interview	Interview with Thurlow Williams, Stone County, Arkansas, by Cuva Williams Neal, 4 July 1977. Transcript prepared by Cuva Neal, copy in possession of Desmond Walls Allen.
Letter	Letter from Alpha M. Williams, 802 Castaic, Oildale, CA 93308, to Desmond Walls Allen, P.O. Box 303, Conway, AR 72033, 22 July 1991. Original in possession of Desmond Allen; Miss Williams is the granddaughter of Harrison Williams.
Manuscript	Pence Funeral Home Records, Conway, Arkansas, Book 3, page 87, Pence Collection, Arkansas History Commission, Little Rock, Ark
Marriage Record	Jones-Smith Marriage, 17 September 1877, Faulkner County Marriage Book 3, p. 72, County Clerk's Office, Conway, Ark.
Military Compiled Service Record (microfilmed)	D.H. Grimes, compiled military service record (Corporal, Company I, 27th Arkansas Infantry, *Compiled Service Records of Confederate Soldiers Who Served in Organizations from the State of Arkansas*, microfilm publication M317, (Washington, D.C.: National Archives), roll 195.
Newspaper	"Aged Resident Dies," (Obituary of Jane Smith), *Izard County Register*, Melbourne, Arkansas, 7 August 1947, page 7, column 2.
Pension File	M.C. (Mrs. James) Aaron Confederate Pension file, 1904, No. 8,997, "Confederate Pension Applications," microfilmed series, Arkansas History Commission, Little Rock.
Photograph	Hannah Grimes Moffitt photograph, original, inscribed on back, "Love from your grandma, Hannah Moffitt," date unknown but appears to have been taken during the last years of her life (death was in 1923), photo is 5" × 7". Gift to Desmond Walls Allen in 1988 from Curtis H. Williams, grandson of Hannah Moffitt.
Probate File	Aaron Hightower probate file no. 2478, County Clerk's office, Faulkner County, Arkansas. John Lancaster entry, Izard County 1851 tax list, Blue Mountain township, no pagination, Izard County microfilm roll no. 7, Arkansas History Commission, Little Rock
URL (Universal Resource Locator)	http://arkansasgravestones.org/cemetery.php?cemID=4487 Herpel Cemetery, Stone County, Arkansas, listing by ArkansasGravestones.org, 15 March 2011 (date the website was last updated).
Will	James Lingo will (1834), Madison County Will Book 1, page 47, County Clerk's Office, Edwardsville, Illinois.

APPENDIX B

RESOURCES

This section lists websites, books, companies, agencies, and products mentioned in *Family History Detective*. It isn't meant as a product endorsement list, just a helpful starting point toward finding the resources and information you need to assist your genealogical research.

Do Internet searches first. Fire up your favorite search engine (such as Google) and key in your search terms. It's helpful to spend some time learning about advanced search techniques that can enhance and speed up your inquiries. URLs change; if one listed here doesn't work, search for the topic. A reminder: There are no spaces in URLs – if it looks like a space, type an underscore.

Check your local library for books, and if they don't have a particular title, request interlibrary loan. Bookstores, both online and in person, can generally find just about any title, new or used.

This section is arranged alphabetically by topic to help you quickly find the references you need. Books and some URLs are written in proper source citation for ease of reference should you use them in your research.

ADOPTION

Books about adoption fall into four broad categories: how-to guides for prospective parents, technical works for social workers, books to help children understand adoption, and genealogy sources. Search by keyword (e.g., "*genealogy adoption research*") in online bookstores. Pay attention to the publication dates and read consumers' reviews. There are many websites devoted to the topic. Avoid the ones that want to sell research services.

Mary J. Rillera, *Adoption Searchbook: Techniques for Tracing People, Third Ed.* (Westminster, Calif.: Triadoption Publications, 1993).

www.genealogy.com/69_taylor.html "All About Adoption Research" by Maureen Taylor, 2011.

Use your favorite Internet search engine to learn more about the adoption laws in effect at the time and place you were born. The situation isn't hopeless; it just takes more work and some time to learn about adoption research.

AUTOBIOGRAPHY

Sunny Morton, *My Life & Times* (Cincinnati, Ohio: Family Tree Books, 2011).

CENSUS RECORDS

You can obtain copies of information from unreleased census records about yourself from the Personal Service Branch, Bureau of the Census, PO Box 1545, Jeffersonville, Ind. 47131. Form BC-600 describes fees and requirements; download it from <www.census.gov/genealogy/www/bc-600.pdf>.

Search federal and state census records on Ancestry.com and FamilySearch.org.

For a book that provides an overview of state census records try:
Ann S. Lainhart, *State Census Records* (Baltimore: Genealogical Publishing Co., 1992).

EVIDENCE EVALUATION

Elizabeth S. Mills, *Evidence! Citation & Analysis for the Family Historian* (Baltimore: Genealogical Publishing Co., Inc., 1997).

Noel C. Stevenson, *Genealogical Evidence: A Guide to the Standard of Proof Relating to Pedigrees, Ancestry, Heirship, and Family History*, Rev. Ed. (Laguna Hills, Calif.: Aegean Park Press, 1989).

FUNERAL HOMES

Several companies maintain online directories of funeral homes in the United States. Do an Internet search for "*Funeral Home directory,*" or "*Funeral Home*" and the place name you're interested in. Check death certificates and newspaper obituaries for funeral home names, then do an Internet search for that establishment.

HANDWRITING

There are many articles, examples, and tutorials online; search for "*deciphering old handwriting.*" If you find a handwritten name or word online in a scanned document that you can't read, use a screen-capture utility such as Snipping Tool, which comes with Windows 7, to grab an image to send to an experienced friend to read. Also send the URL where you found the source so your helper can compare words and letters from the entire source.

E. Kay Kirkham, *How to Read the Handwriting and Records of Early America* (Salt Lake City: Deseret Book Co., 1961).

HEIRLOOMS

Don Williams and Louisa Jaggar, *Saving Stuff: How to Care for and Preserve Your Collectibles, Heirlooms, and Other Prized Possessions* (New York: Fireside, 2005).

Jane S. Long and Richard W. Long, *Caring for Your Family Treasures: A Concise Guide to Caring for Your Cherished Belongings* (New York: Harry N. Abrams, Inc., 2000).

HOUSES

Sally Light, *House Histories: A Guide to Tracing the Genealogy of Your Home* (Spencertown, New York: Golden Hill Press, Inc., 1993).

Virginia McAlester and Lee McAlester, *A Field Guide to American Houses* (New York: Alfred A. Knopf, 1995).

INTERNET

One of the most comprehensive collections of links to genealogical websites is **Cyndi's List** <www.cyndislist.com>.

Some of the best places to start an online search are:

Ancestry.com <www.ancestry.com>

FamilySearch.org <www.familysearch.org>, the Family History Library's website

HeritageQuestOnline <www.heritagequestonline.com> (but you must enter through a library portal)

INTERVIEWING PEOPLE

www.familytreemagazine.com/article/20-questions "20 Questions for Interviewing Relatives" *Family Tree Magazine,* 21 July 2012.

LAND RECORDS

Search the Internet for *"rectangular survey system"* or *"metes and bounds survey system."* Or search for *"land records"* and your particular place of interest.

E. Wade Hone, *Land & Property Research in the United States* (Salt Lake City: Ancestry, Inc., 1997).

LEGAL TERMS

An indispensable reference for understanding cryptic words in old legal documents is:

Henry Campbell Black, *Black's Law Dictionary: Definitions of the Terms and Phrases of American and English Jurisprudence, Ancient and Modern,* revised 4th ed. (St. Paul, Minn.: West Publishing Co., 1968)

Go to <www.google.com/books> and search for *"black's law dictionary free"* to find older editions you can use free online.

LIBRARIES

The Family History Library, 35 N. West Temple St., Salt Lake City, UT 84150, is the largest genealogical library in the world. You can access many of its holdings by visiting a local FamilySearch Center. To find one near you, visit <www.familysearch.org/locations>.

For descriptions of some of the best genealogy libraries in the United States see:

familytreemagazine.com/article/9-libraries "9 Genealogy Libraries to Visit Before You Die" by Lauren Gamber, *Family Tree Magazine,* 28 September 2009.

Most large libraries have established websites. To check for a particular library, enter its name in any search engine. To find mailing addresses for libraries, check online or find this book in the reference section of your local library, there's a new edition published each year:

R.R. Bowker, *American Library Directory* (New Providence, NJ: Reed Reference Publishing).

MAGAZINES

Go to <www.familytreemagazine.com> to learn about *Family Tree Magazine*. Read timely articles about new tips and trends in genealogical research.

MAPS

The **U.S. Geological Survey (USGS) Geographic Names Information System** (GNIS) database is available for searches on the Internet: <http://geonames.usgs.gov/>. To order topographic maps produced by the USGS visit <http://topomaps.usgs.gov/ordering_maps.html>. The Federal Highway Administration maintains a list of links to state highway departments at <http://www.fhwa.dot.gov/webstate.htm>.

The Library of Congress in Washington, DC, has a tremendous collection of maps. Much of their catalog is online and available through the Internet. Start here: <http://international.loc.gov/ammem/gmdhtml/gmdhome.html> for information about the digitized part of their collection.

For an overview of the National Archives' map collection go to <http://www.archives.gov/publications/finding-aids/maps/>.

Other lists of place names, called "gazetteers," are available for a wide range of regions and time periods. *Omni Gazetteer of the United States of America*, an 11-volume set published by Omnigraphics is a comprehensive reference tool found in many libraries.

FamilyHistory101.com offers online access to maps illustrating changing county boundaries in the United States at <http://www.familyhistory101.com/maps.html>.

For current place names, of course, Google Maps <maps.google.com> is at your fingertips. If you download Google Earth <earth.google.com>, you can view historic maps for some areas with the "layers" function. Bing Maps <www.bing.com/maps> is an alternative to Google Maps.

A GPS (global positioning system) device, either stand-alone or in a smart phone, is an excellent tool for genealogists.

Editors of *Family Tree Magazine, Family Tree Sourcebook* (Cincinnati, Ohio: Family Tree Books, 2010). This book lists all the counties in all the states and gives their creation dates and a description of the territory from which they were created.

Kenneth T. Jackson, ed., *Atlas of American History* (New York: Charles Scribners' Sons, 1943, 1978). There are several books with this title, search for this particular one as it's excellent.

Randall D. Sale and Edwin D. Karn, *American Expansion: A Book of Maps* (Lincoln, Neb.: University of Nebraska Press, 1962). This thin volume shows settlement patterns and public land offices.

William Thorndale and William Dollarhide. *Map Guide to the U.S. Federal Censuses, 1790-1920* (Baltimore, Md.: Genealogical Publishing Co., 1987).

MEDICAL CONSIDERATIONS

Carol Krause, *How Healthy Is Your Family Tree?: A Complete Guide to Tracing Your Family's Medical and Behavioral History* (New York: Simon and Schuster, 1995).

MILITARY RECORDS

Military service records for people who served in the armed forces in the last seventy-five years are protected by privacy laws. Most of these records are housed at the National Personnel Records Center, 9700 Page Blvd., St. Louis, MO 63132. However, under the 1974 Freedom of Information Law, some data from the records can be released to people other than the serviceperson. Read more about it at <www.archives.gov/st-louis>.

Military records from pre-twentieth-century wars are housed at the National Archives. Request copies of these records following the information on this site: <www.archives.gov/veterans/military-service-records/pre-ww-1-records.html>.

James W. Oberly, *Sixty Million Acres: American Veterans and the Public Lands Before the Civil War* (Kent, Ohio: Kent State University Press, 1990).

PHOTOGRAPHS

To learn more about using photos in your family history research, go to the Photo Detective blog: blog.familytreemagazine.com/photodetectiveblog Photo Detective by Maureen A. Taylor, day monthy year (date of post).

Maureen A. Taylor, *Preserving Your Family Photographs* (Massachusetts: Picture Perfect Press, 2010).

PRESERVATION OF DOCUMENTS

Gaylord Brothers, Inc., PO Box 4901, Syracuse, NY 13221, <www.gaylord.com> is a library supplier with a line of archivally safe boxes, folders, cleaning supplies, plastic paper clips, and Abbey pH Pens to test for acid content in paper.

Hollinger Metal Edge, 6340 Bandini Blvd., Commerce, CA 90040, 800-862-2228, and 9401 Northeast Dr., Fredericksburg, VA 22408, (800) 634-0491 <www.hollingermetaledge.com> offers a wide variety of archival safe products including boxes, folders, tissue paper and pens.

PUBLISHING A FAMILY HISTORY

Learn more about writing your family history in the Family Tree University course "Creating a Family History Book: Start-to-Finish Guidance for Assembling and Printing a Family Keepsake." This four-week, online class helps you plan, gather and use images and research your book before walking your through the self publishing process. Learn more and register for the class at <www. familytreeuniversity.com/creating-a-family-history-book>.

Patricia Law Hatcher, *Producing a Quality Family History* (Salt Lake City: Ancestry, Inc., 1996).

SELF-DIRECTED LEARNING

Ronald Gross, *The Independent Scholar's Handbook* (Berkeley, Calif.: Ten Speed Press, 1993).

Ronald Gross, *Peak Learning: How to Create Your Own Lifelong Education Program for Personal Enjoyment and Professional Success* (Los Angeles: Jeremy P. Tarcher, Inc., 1991).

SOCIAL HISTORY

Thousands of titles could be listed in this section; the following volumes are only a few examples. For more information about searching for information on specific topics, see:

Francis Paul Prucha, *Handbook for Research in American History: A Guide to Bibliographies and Other Reference Works,* 2nd ed., revised (Lincoln, Neb.: University of Nebraska Press, 1994).

Ray Allen Billington, *Westward Expansion: A History of the American Frontier* (New York: The Macmillian Co., 1949). This volume has been through several editions—check libraries and used bookstores.

Daniel J. Boorstin, *The Americans: The Colonial Experience (*New York: Random House, 1958). Paperback editions of all three volumes are still in print and really cheap on Amazon.com.

Daniel J. Boorstin, *The Americans: The Democratic Experience* (New York: Random House, 1973).

Daniel J. Boorstin, *The Americans: The National Experience* (New York: Random House, 1965).

James K. Crissman, *Death and Dying in Central Appalachia: Changing Attitudes and Practices* (Urbana, Ill.: University of Illinois Press, 1994).

David Hackett Fischer, *Albion's Seed: Four British Folkways in America* (New York: Oxford University Press, 1989).

Lawrence M. Friedman, *A History of American Law,* 2nd ed. (New York: Simon and Schuster, 1985).

Robert W. Habenstein and William M. Lamers, *The History of American Funeral Directing* (Milwaukee, Wisc.: Bulfin Printers, Inc., 1955).

David Freeman Hawke, *Everyday Life in Early America* (New York: Harper and Row, 1988).

James G. Leyburn, *The Scotch-Irish: A Social History* (Chapel Hill, N.C.: University of North Carolina Press, 1962).

Grady McWhiney, *Cracker Culture: Celtic Ways in the Old South.* (Tuscaloosa, Ala.: The University of Alabama Press, 1988).

Ted Morgan, *A Shovel of Stars: The Making of the American West 1800 to the Present* (New York: Simon and Schuster, 1995).

Ted Morgan. *Wilderness at Dawn: The Settling of the North American Continent* (New York: Simon and Schuster, 1993).

Robert W. Ramsey, *Carolina Cradle: Settlement of the Northwest Carolina Frontier, 1747-1762* (Chapel Hill, N.C.: University of North Carolina Press, 1964).

David Charles Sloane, *The Last Great Necessity: Cemeteries in American History* (Baltimore, Md.: The Johns Hopkins Univ. Press, 1991).

Thomas Sowell, *Ethnic America: A History* (New York: Basic Books, 1981). Covers Irish, German, Jewish, Italian, Chinese, Japanese, Blacks, Puerto Ricans, and Mexicans.

SOCIAL SECURITY ADMINISTRATION

Social Security's death index is available from several free sources including <ssdi.rootsweb.ancestry.com>. If you find someone of interest, you can order a copy of Form SS-5, the form filled out by a person to obtain a Social Security card, at <secure.ssa.gov/apps9/eFOIA-FEWeb/internet/main.jsp>.

SOFTWARE

For Windows:

Ancestrial Quest, manufacturer: Incline Software, <www.ancquest.com>

Brother's Keeper, manufacturer: John Steed, <www.bkwin.net>

Family Tree Builder, manufacturer: MyHeritage, <www.myheritage.com>/family-tree-builder>

Family Tree Legends, manufacturer: Pearl Street Software, <www.familytreelegends.com>

Family Tree Maker, manufactured by Ancestry.com, <www.familytreemaker.com> (also for Mac)

Genbox Family History, manufacturer: Thoughtful Creations, <www.genbox.com>

Legacy Family Tree, manufacturer: Millennia Corp., <www.legacyfamilytree.com>

The Master Genealogist, manufacturer: Wholly Genes, <www.whollygenes.com>

Personal Ancestral File, manufacturer: FamilySearch, <www.familysearch.org/eng/paf>

RootsMagic, manufacturer: RootsMagic, Inc,. <www.rootsmagic.com>

For Mac

GEDitCOM II, manufacturer: John A. Nairn, <www.geditcom.com>

Heredis Mac X.2, manufacturer: BSD Concept, <www.myheredis.com>

iFamily for Leopard, manufacturer: Keith Wilson, <www.ifamilyforleopard.com>

MacFamilyTree, manufacturer: Synium Software, <www.syniumsoftware.com/macfamilytree>

Reunion 9, manufacturer: Leister Productions, <www.leisterpro.com>

SOURCE CITATION

Elizabeth S. Mills, *Evidence! Citation & Analysis for the Family Historian* (Baltimore, Md.: Genealogical Publishing Co., Inc., 1997).

The Chicago Manual of Style, 16th Ed. (Chicago: University of Chicago Press, 2010).

VITAL RECORDS

To locate state vital records offices, see the government's Center for Disease Control website, <http://www.cdc.gov/nchs/w2w.htm>. (For births and deaths in foreign countries, do an Internet search to find the national site, then follow the links to smaller political entities.)

WRITING SKILLS

If you need help with your writing skills, consider the "Write Your Family History" online course offered by Family Tree University, <www.familytreeuniversity.com/write-your-family-history-create-a-captivating-record-of-your-familys-story>. You can also take a composition class at a local college, or fortify yourself with some good books on the topic.

Charles T. Brusaw, Gerald J. Alred, and Walter E. Oliu, *The Business Writer's Handbook,* 4th revised ed. (New York: St. Martin's Press, 1993). Also published as *Handbook of Technical Writing*; presents five steps to successful writing: preparation, research, organization, writing, and revision.

Claire Kehrwald Cook, *The MLA's Line by Line: How to Edit Your Own Writing* (Boston: Houghton Mifflin Co., 1985). Includes advice from an editor on "loose, baggy sentences, faulty connections, ill-matched partners" and other writing problems.

Richard Lederer and Richard Dowis, *The Write Way: The S.P.E.L.L.* Guide to Real-Life Writing.* (New York: Pocket Books, 1995). [* Society for the Preservation of English Language and Literature; humorous approach.]

William Zinsser, *On Writing Well, 30th Anniversary Edition: The Classic Guide to Writing Nonfiction* (New York: Harper and Row, 2006).

APPENDIX C

Forms

Family Group Sheet of the

_____ Family

	SOURCE #		SOURCE #
Full Name of Husband		Birth Date and Place	
His Father		Marriage Date and Place	
His Mother with Maiden Name		Death Date and Place	
		Burial	
Full Name of Wife		Birth Date and Place	
Her Father		Death Date and Place	
Her Mother with Maiden Name		Burial	
Other Spouses		Marriage Date and Place	

Children of This Marriage	Birth Date and Place	Death Date, Place and Burial	Marriage Date, Place and Spouse

FIVE-GENERATION ANCESTOR CHART

Chart # ____
1 on this chart = ____ on chart # ____

see chart #

1

birth date and place

marriage date and place

death date and place

spouse

2

birth date and place

marriage date and place

death date and place

3

birth date and place

death date and place

4

birth date and place

marriage date and place

death date and place

5

birth date and place

death date and place

6

birth date and place

marriage date and place

death date and place

7

birth date and place

death date and place

8

birth date and place

marriage date and place

death date and place

9

birth date and place

death date and place

10

birth date and place

marriage date and place

death date and place

11

birth date and place

death date and place

12

birth date and place

death date and place

13

birth date and place

marriage date and place

death date and place

14

birth date and place

death date and place

15

birth date and place

death date and place

16

17

18

19

20

21

22

23

24

25

26

27

28

29

30

31

Research Calendar

Note the records you've checked for ancestral clues.

Researcher: _____ Ancestor: _____

Locality: _____ Time Period: _____

Brief Problem Statement: _____

SEARCH DATE	WHERE AVAILABLE	CALL #	TITLE/AUTHOR/ PUBLISHER/YEAR OR RECORD IDENTIFICATION INFORMATION	NOTES	PAGE #s

INDEX

FREE DOWNLOAD

FILL-IN FAMILY HISTORY FORMS

Track your research with electronic versions of the worksheets found in this book. Type information directly on the PDF forms, print them for reference and update with new discoveries. This download includes a bonus decorative family tree suitable for framing.

Visit **<familytreeuniversity.com/fill-in-forms>**

Trace Your Roots with Family Tree Books

Family Tree Legacies
by The editors of
Family Tree Magazine

My Life & Times
by Sunny Morton

The Family Tree Source book
by The editors of
Family Tree Magazine

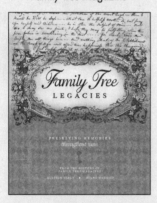

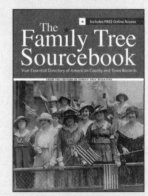

Available at your favorite bookstore, online booksellers and **<shopfamilytree.com>**

FAMILY
TREE
BOOKS

Like us for special offers and giveaways:
<facebook.com/familytreemagazine>

HARRISON COUNTY PUBLIC LIBRARY

3 ELIZ 60002143 L